INSTRUCTOR'S MANUAL

Intermediate Level

LISTENING TO COMMUNICATE IN ENGLISH

Virginia Nelson

National Textbook Company
a division of *NTC Publishing Group* • Lincolnwood, Illinois USA

About the Author

Virginia Nelson is a lecturer in the Summer Session ESL Program at Cornell University and a curriculum writer for a Title VII science-based whole literacy program in Tempe, Arizona.

Published by National Textbook Company, a division of NTC Publishing Group.
© 1997 by NTC Publishing Group, 4255 West Touhy Avenue,
Lincolnwood (Chicago), Illinois 60646-1975 U.S.A.
All rights reserved. No part of this book may be reproduced,
stored in a retrieval system, or transmitted in any form or by any means,
electronic, mechanical, photocopying, recording or otherwise, without
the prior permission of NTC Publishing Group.
Manufactured in the United States of America.

7 8 9 ML 0 9 8 7 6 5 4 3 2 1

Contents

Introduction v
  Vocabulary Selection v
  Structure Selection v
  Presentation of the Material vi

Strategies for Classroom Use viii

Extension and Practice Activities ix

Tapescript xi

Unit 1
Lesson 1: I Am Happy That I Have a Sister 1
Lesson 2: I Am Not Chinese 4
Lesson 3: He Paints Houses for a Living, and Hates It 6
Lesson 4: You Always Look Tired 9
Lesson 5: They Don't Even Have a Movie Theater 11
Lesson 6: Anything Else? 14
Lesson 7: Can You Draw a Stegosaurus? 16
Lesson 8: Does the Sun Ever Come Out in Bergen? 18
Lesson 9: I Am Not Cut Out for Parachuting 21
Lesson 10: Call Back Later 23

Unit 2
Lesson 11: I Ate Too Much Pizza 26
Lesson 12: I Got a Cordless Phone for $6.99! 28
Lesson 13: Where Did You Buy Your Down Jacket? 30
Lesson 14: How Did You Break Your Elbow? 32
Lesson 15: This Soup Is Awful! Did You Forget the Salt? 34

Unit 3
Lesson 16: I Won't Be Back until August 36
Lesson 17: You Don't Play Football! 38
Lesson 18: I'm Going to Quit 39
Lesson 19: Are You Going to Go Back to Your Country? 42
Lesson 20: Why Won't You Lend Me Three Thousand Dollars? 44

Unit 4
Lesson 21: We Got a New Teacher Yesterday 46
Lesson 22: I Came to Register My Brother 48
Lesson 23: Are You Going to Buy a Wheelchair or Rent One? 51
Lesson 24: If You Don't Open Your Mouth and Answer Me,
           I'm Leaving! 53
Lesson 25: A Pain in My Shoulder, an Earache, and My Arm Hurts 56
Lesson 26: I Won't Say Hello Because She Never Says Hello 59
Lesson 27: Did You Read the Book I Gave You? 62
Lesson 28: Did You Tell Them We Are Not Inviting Them? 64
Lesson 29: Did She Say Why She Is Moving? 66
Lesson 30: The Winter County Free Public Library 68

Answer Key 73

Introduction

Listening to Communicate in English is a language acquisition/communication improvement kit for intermediate students of English. Each of the thirty lessons in the program provides practice in hearing American English, understanding what has been heard, and reacting to the message. The final exercises in each lesson give students the opportunity to demonstrate and evaluate how much of the message they have understood.

Listening to Communicate in English exposes students to normally paced American English conversation. Careful selection and sequencing of vocabulary and structures prevent students from getting discouraged and feeling overwhelmed about all the elements involved in mastering conversation in English. In addition, a great deal of repetition and practice is built into the materials to give students the assurance that they *can* understand spoken English and respond to it.

Students have ample opportunity to practice each skill they need to develop. They evaluate their own work, thus avoiding the threat of a test. Some of the exercises encourage students to practice with other students and with the teacher to enhance the friendly, supportive nature of the communicative classroom. Thus, students get their first practice in producing the designated structures while still in the secure classroom environment.

Listening to Communicate in English consists of four high-quality cassette tapes, a student workbook, and an instructor's manual containing a complete tapescript and answer key. A stand-alone answer key is also available. The cassette/workbook format of the program permits students who want or need additional practice to work alone. *Listening to Communicate in English* can therefore be used effectively for self-study as well as in the language classroom. With their presentation of native-speaker role models, the cassettes are especially useful for classes in which the teacher is not a native speaker of English.

Listening to Communicate in English is appropriate for students who have almost no acquaintance with spoken English; students who have completed a beginning course; students with extensive reading, writing, and structure training who cannot understand spoken English or respond to it; and native speakers of English who find it difficult to communicate effectively.

Vocabulary Selection

Although the real world does not select vocabulary to meet the acquisition levels of listeners, *Listening to Communicate in English* does. Each of the thirty conversations is a retelling of an actual conversation heard by the author. For the purposes of this program, unusual words and expressions have been replaced by their more common synonyms. For example, *unhappy* replaced *depressed* and *down*. *Beans* replaced *lentils*. In this manner, students are provided with lexical items they can use in the widest possible range of situations, from which they will later acquire more specialized vocabularies to deal effectively with specific subjects that interest them.

Structure Selection

Like vocabulary, structures are not presented in natural conversations with native speakers of English in such a way as to guide students from the simple through the compound verb tenses. However, English and communications instructors find great advantages to using materials that focus on one structure at a time.

Many instructors are expected to write lesson plans and objectives to document their work. Using grammatically structured materials makes stating objectives and writing plans an easier task, allowing more time for the business of teaching and creating a communicative classroom. Another advantage to using structured materials is that many students expect to learn structure by structure. They feel more comfortable working on "Structure A" this week than on a general mishmash of English, even though such a mishmash may be closer to the real world.

Presentation of the Material

The thirty lessons in *Listening to Communicate in English* are grouped into four units. The conversations in Unit 1 focus on actions in the present. Unit 2 focuses on actions in the past, while Unit 3 focuses on actions in the future. Unit 4 reviews and reinforces the skills and structures presented in the first three units.

In addition, the lessons are sequenced by the subject and style of the conversations. Conversations with a heavier sociolinguistic load are presented in the last half of the course, while the earlier lessons are simpler to comprehend. The first nine lessons, for example, contain no difficult or unusual situations. Lesson 10 is the first presentation of something typically American: how an adolescent boy addresses the mother of a friend. In Lesson 12, sister criticizes brother. In Lesson 15, two men are involved in cooking. A perusal of later lessons will demonstrate increasing hints of only-in-America behavior. An example is Lesson 20, in which one brother suggests that the other postpone repaying a loan to their father.

Finally, Lesson 30 is designed to insure student success. It is somewhat easier than the previous lessons, both in structures and in sociolinguistic load. It is positioned at the end of the program to help students see that they have improved, and to reinforce their ability and desire to communicate effectively in English.

Within each unit, the lesson exercises follow a specific pattern. Exercises involving the same skills are spiraled throughout the lessons in order to vary the task sequence. Below is an overview of the types of exercises included in each unit:

Unit 1

Exercise 1: Writing dictated sentences with most of each answer supplied, to build confidence and provide practice in hearing and writing discrete structures

Exercise 2: Demonstrating basic understanding by answering multiple-choice comprehension questions

Exercise 3: Reviewing stressed and unstressed words from the conversation by filling in the blanks

Exercise 4: Practicing a single structure, with most of each answer supplied

Exercise 5: Demonstrating comprehension by answering factual yes-no questions

Exercise 6: Identifying the order of events to review the conversation
Exercise 7: Practicing writing a specific structure with oral cues
Exercise 8: Writing a partial synthesis of the conversation with written and oral cues

Unit 2
Exercise 1: Writing questions from dictation
Exercise 2: Demonstrating comprehension by answering factual yes-no questions
Exercise 3: Writing or completing short answers to oral questions
Exercise 4: Associating information with questions used to obtain that information
Exercise 5: Practicing writing a specific structure with oral cues
Exercise 6: Demonstrating basic understanding by answering multiple-choice comprehension questions
Exercise 7: Sequencing events from the conversation with written cues

Unit 3
Exercise 1: Demonstrating comprehension by answering factual yes-no questions
Exercise 2: Demonstrating basic understanding by answering multiple-choice comprehension questions
Exercises
3 and 4: Completing lesson-specific exercises that incorporate graphic and tabulating tasks, selecting correct information or endings, and other sorting operations based on the conversation
Exercise 5: Practicing writing a single structure with oral cues in statement form
Exercise 6: Practicing writing a single structure with oral cues in question form

Unit 4
Exercise 1: Studying words and their definitions for vocabulary review and enrichment
Exercise 2: Identifying words from their definitions
Exercise 3: Writing answers to oral comprehension questions
Exercise 4: Reviewing the conversation by filling in missing words from dictation
Exercise 5: Demonstrating basic understanding by answering multiple-choice comprehension questions
Exercise 6: Identifying true and false statements
Exercise 7: Fine-tuning early intermediate listening skills by identifying a spoken statement in writing
Exercise 8: Paraphrasing
Exercise 9: Integrating additional language applications such as speaking and illustrating to practice skills and demonstrate comprehension
Exercise 10: Self-evaluating of comprehension and improvement

Strategies for Classroom Use

The basic procedure for using the program is self-evident: the instructor or student need only turn on the cassette and open the book. However, instructors may wish to increase the level of communication in the classroom by following a procedure such as the following for each lesson.

- Students read the lesson title and the introductory comment.
- They listen to both on the cassette.
- One person rephrases the introductory comment.
- Students listen to the conversation. (Watching the meter setting on the cassette player facilitates returning to the beginning of the conversation if students require a second listening.)
- Students retell the important parts of the conversation.
- The instructor asks student to make comparisons between events in the conversation and similar situations in their homelands.
- Students complete the exercises, stopping after each one. (At the instructor's discretion, students may listen to the conversation again before completing any difficult exercises.)
- The instructor walks around during each exercise to informally assess the level of difficulty.
- Students correct each exercise before continuing. If many students had trouble with a particular exercise, the instructor replays crucial lines or sections of the conversation that many students might have misunderstood.
- Students create and role-play a similar conversation.

After the students have listened to each conversation, instructors may wish to ask the following questions:

1. Who are the people involved in this situation?
2. What would be different about this situation if it happened in your homeland?
3. Tell one feature of this conversation that surprises you.
4. Ask one question about this conversation. Make sure that the answer is in the conversation.
5. Ask one question about this conversation. Make sure that the answer is *not* in the conversation.

Extension and Practice Activities

The most valuable extension and practice activities for *Listening to Communicate in English* are those in which students integrate listening, speaking, reading, and writing skills. Below is a list of suggested activities for use after any lesson:

1. Write a similar conversation involving people in your class. Choose students to modify your dialogue. After the whole class checks their work, choose students to read the conversation.

2. Ask each student to write three questions about your conversation (see Activity 1 above). The rest of the class should be able to answer the questions by reading your conversation.

3. Ask each student to write three questions that *cannot* be answered by reading your conversation (see Activity 1 above).

4. Have the students write letters to one of the speakers in the lesson conversation. Each letter should ask two questions. Let the students exchange letters with a classmate and answer each other's questions.

5. Have the students illustrate the conversation and write captions for their illustrations.

6. At the end of a unit, have the class make a chart showing *who, what, where, when,* and *how* for the conversation in each lesson. For how many conversations can they answer all five questions?

7. Have the students try writing free-form poems to explain what happens in a conversation. They should make their poems as humorous as they can, and try to make the class laugh as they read their poems aloud.

8. Group the students to read the conversation with others in the class. Record their reading. Let them evaluate how they sound.

9. Take the students on a short field trip to an appropriate location where they can practice what they learned in the lesson (e.g., to a day care center or a bakery for Lesson 1; to the school office for Lesson 2).

10. Have the students keep a log of their progress through the program. Each time they complete a lesson, have them record the date, note whether they enjoyed the topic or not, and describe the topic briefly. In addition, they should tell where they might use the new information outside the classroom and make notes on their satisfaction with the work they did in the lesson.

Tapescript

About This Tapescript

Pauses between exercise items have been included in the recorded material. However, since the amount of time it takes to complete an item within an exercise will vary from student to student, use of the pause button is recommended whenever necessary. There is no prescribed amount of time in which students must complete an exercise. In addition, some exercises may require more than one listening. In other exercises, students may listen to the recorded material and then complete the exercise based on the information they have in their books.

Unit 1

Lesson 1: I Am Happy That I Have a Sister *page 3*

  Noah is three. Karah is nine months. Is Noah happy?

Father: Noah, stop hitting Karah.
Noah: I am not hitting Karah.
Father: Yes, you are.
Noah: No, I am not.
Father: Stop it right now.
Noah: No.
Father: Give Karah your hand.
Noah: Why?
Father: Help her up.
Noah: She can't walk.
Father: She can stand.
Noah: I can walk.
Father: You can walk. You can run.
Noah: I am a big boy.
Father: Give Karah your hand.
Noah: No.
Father: Come here, Karah.
Noah: She can't walk.
Father: She can crawl.
Noah: Turtles crawl.
Father: Babies crawl, too. Karah, come here. I have a muffin for you.
Noah: A muffin?
Father: Yes, they are from your cousin Roberta. She wants Karah to try some banana muffins.
Noah: Can I have one?
Father: Sure you can.
Noah: I am happy that I have a sister!

1. a. What do you know about Noah? Write what you hear.
    1. He is a boy.
    2. He is Karah's brother.
    3. He is three.
    4. He is hitting Karah.
    5. He can walk.
    6. He can talk.

b. What do you know about Karah? Write what you hear.
   1. She is a girl.
   2. She is Noah's sister.
   3. She is nine months old.
   4. She is a baby.
   5. She can crawl.
   6. She can stand.
   7. She cannot walk.
   8. She can eat muffins.

c. What do you know about Roberta? Write what you hear.
   1. She is Noah's cousin.
   2. She is Karah's cousin.
   3. She can bake.
   4. She wants Karah to eat muffins.

2. Listen to the questions. Underline the correct answer for each question.
   a. Who is Noah?
   b. Who is Karah?
   c. Who is three years old?
   d. Who is nine months old?
   e. Who can bake banana muffins?
   f. Karah can't walk. Why not?
   g. Noah wants a banana muffin. Why?
   h. Noah says, "I am a big boy." Why?
   i. Karah can't walk. What *can* she do?
   j. Whom should Noah give his hand to?

3. Look at these words. Listen to the sentences. Put the correct word on each line.
   a. Noah is three.
   b. Yes, you are.
   c. Give Karah your hand.
   d. Help her up.
   e. She can't walk.
   f. She can stand.
   g. I can walk.
   h. You can run.
   i. Come here, Karah.
   j. I have a muffin for you.
   k. She wants Karah to try some banana muffins.
   l. Can I have one?

4. Karah is a baby. She can't do many things. Ask why not.
   a. Why can't Karah walk?
   b. Why can't Karah talk?
   c. Why can't Karah bake banana muffins?
   d. Why can't Karah help Noah up?
   e. Why can't Karah help Roberta up?

5. Listen to these questions. Circle **yes** or **no**.
   a. Can Noah talk?
   b. Can Karah talk?
   c. Can Noah walk?
   d. Can Karah walk?
   e. Can Roberta bake banana muffins?
   f. Can Karah try banana muffins?
   g. Can Karah help Noah up?
   h. Can Noah help Karah up?

6. You will hear the statements. Write numbers to show the correct order.
   a. Noah is hitting Karah
      Noah asks for a banana muffin.
   b. Noah crawls.
      Noah walks.
   c. Noah says he is a big boy.
      Noah wants a banana muffin.
   d. Noah is hitting Karah.
      Noah says he is happy he has a sister.
   e. Noah is hitting Karah.
      Noah says turtles crawl.

7. Listen to these sentences.
   - Turtles crawl.
   - Babies crawl, too.
   - Karah crawls.

   Look at the **s** in "Karah crawls." Listen to the statements. Then write a statement with Karah's name. Use an **s**.
   a. Babies stand.
      Boys stand, too.
   b. Girls hit.
      Boys hit, too.
   c. Turtles eat.
      Babies eat, too.
   d. Turtles sit in the sun.
      Babies sit in the sun, too.
   e. Girls eat banana muffins.
      Boys eat banana muffins, too.

8. Write what you know about Noah, Karah, and Roberta.
   a. Noah is a boy.
   b. Noah likes muffins.
   c. Karah eats muffins.
   d. Karah is a baby.
   e. Roberta is Noah's cousin.
   f. Roberta can bake muffins.

Lesson 2: I Am Not Chinese *page 8*

Rose Wong is in class at Central School. She studies English at night. Someone calls her to the office. Does Rose speak Chinese?

Voice over p.a. system: Rose Wong, please come to the office.
(sound of footsteps through a hall)
Rose: Hello.
Office worker: Hello, Mrs. Wong. I am sorry to take you out of your English class.
Rose: No problem.
Office worker: This is Mr. Chen. He speaks Chinese. He wants some information. Can you help us?
Rose: How can I help you?
Office worker: Please ask Mr. Chen what information he wants.
Rose: I don't speak Chinese. I speak Spanish.
Office worker: Your name is Wong.
Rose: My husband is Chinese.
Office worker: You look Chinese.
Rose: My father is a Quechua Indian, and my mother is Mexican.
Office worker: Oh, I am sorry!
Rose: That is okay. It happens all the time.

1. a. What do you know about Rose Wong? Write what you hear.
    1. She is in class.
    2. She is at Central School.
    3. She is studying.
    4. Her husband is Chinese.
    5. Her father is a Quechua Indian.
    6. Her mother is Mexican.
    7. She is not Chinese.
    8. She does not speak Chinese.
    9. She speaks Spanish.
    10. She looks Chinese.

   b. What do you know about Mr. Chen? Write what you hear.
    1. He is at Central School.
    2. He is in the office.
    3. He speaks Chinese.
    4. He wants some information.

   c. What do you know about Central School? Write what you hear.
    1. There are classes there.
    2. There are English classes there.
    3. Rose studies there.
    4. Mr. Chen studies there.
    5. Central School is open at night.
    6. The office is open at night.

2. Listen to the questions. Underline the correct answer for each question.
   a. Where is Rose Wong?
   b. What is Rose Wong studying?
   c. Where is Mr. Chen?
   d. What does Mr. Chen speak?
   e. What does Mr. Chen want?
   f. What does Rose speak?
   g. Who speaks Quechua?
   h. Who is a Quechua Indian?
   i. Who is Chinese?

3. Look at these words. Listen to the sentences. Put the correct word on each line.
   a. Rose Wong is in class.
   b. She studies English.
   c. Please come to the office.
   d. I am sorry to take you out of your class.
   e. This is Mr. Chen.
   f. He speaks Chinese.
   g. He wants some information.
   h. Can you help us?
   i. How can I help you?
   j. Please ask Mr. Chen what he wants.
   k. I don't speak Chinese.
   l. I speak Spanish.
   m. Your name is Wong.
   n. You look Chinese.
   o. It happens all the time.

4. Ask questions about Rose and Mr. Chen. Use **can** or **does**.
   a. Does Rose study English?
   b. Does Rose go to the office?
   c. Can Mr. Chen speak English?
   d. Can Mr. Chen speak Chinese?
   e. Does Mr. Chen want information?
   f. Can Rose help Mr. Chen?
   g. Can Rose speak Chinese?

5. Listen to these questions. Circle **yes** or **no**.
   a. Does Rose study English?
   b. Does Mr. Chen speak Chinese?
   c. Does he speak English?
   d. Can Rose speak Chinese?
   e. Can she speak Spanish?
   f. Can Rose help Mr. Chen?

6. You will hear two statements. Write numbers to show the correct order.
   a. Rose is in class.
      Rose is in the office.
   b. Rose goes to the office.
      Rose says her husband is Chinese.
   c. Rose goes to her English class at night.
      Rose goes to the office.
   d. Mr. Chen goes to the office.
      Mr. Chen asks for information.
   e. Rose goes to the office
      Rose says she does not speak Chinese.

7. Listen to these sentences.
   - Rose speaks Spanish.
   - She doesn't speak Chinese.

   Look at the **s** in "Rose speaks Spanish." Look at the **doesn't** in "She **doesn't** speak Chinese." Listen to the statement. Then write a statement with "Japanese." Use **doesn't**.
   a. Mr. Chen speaks Chinese.
   b. Rose's husband speaks Chinese.
   c. Rose's father speaks Quechua.
   d. Rose's mother speaks Spanish.
   e. Mrs. Wong speaks Spanish.
   f. Mr. Wong speaks English and Chinese.
   g. Mr. Smith speaks French.

8. Write what you know about Rose Wong, her husband, her mother, her father, and Mr. Chen.
   a. Rose studies English.
   b. Rose goes to school at night.
   c. Rose's husband is Chinese.
   d. Rose's father is Quechua.
   e. Rose's mother speaks Spanish.
   f. Mr. Chen speaks Chinese.

Lesson 3: He Paints Houses for a Living, and Hates It   *page 13*

Terry and Lucy live on the same street. Terry sees Lucy outside, and he stops to talk to her. What does Lucy's dad do?

Terry: Hi, Lucy. What's wrong?

Lucy: I don't know. Nothing, really.

Terry: You don't look happy.

Lucy: I don't feel happy. And my dad doesn't feel happy either.

Terry: What's wrong with your dad?

Lucy: His job, again—too much work, not enough money.

Terry: What does he do, anyway? Teach school?

Lucy: No.

Terry: Does he load trucks? He looks strong.

Lucy: No. He paints houses for a living, and hates it.

1. a. What do you know about Lucy? Write what you hear.
      1. She looks unhappy.
      2. She doesn't look happy.
      3. She doesn't feel happy.
      4. She feels unhappy.
   b. What do you know about Lucy's father? Write what you hear.
      1. He doesn't feel happy.
      2. He feels unhappy.
      3. He has too much work.
      4. He doesn't have enough money.
      5. He doesn't teach school.
      6. He doesn't load trucks.
      7. He paints houses.
      8. He hates his job.
   c. What do you know about Terry? Write what you hear.
      1. He lives near Lucy.
      2. He sees Lucy outside.
      3. He stops to talk to her.

2. Listen to the questions. Underline the correct answer for each question.
   a. Where do Lucy and Terry live?
   b. How does Lucy look?
   c. How does Lucy's dad feel?
   d. What is wrong with Lucy's dad's job?
   e. What does Lucy's dad do?
   f. How does Lucy's dad feel about his job?

3. Look at these words. Listen to the sentences. Put the correct word on each line.
   a. What is wrong?
   b. I don't know.
   c. You don't look happy.
   d. I don't feel happy.
   e. He doesn't feel happy, either.
   f. He has too much work.
   g. What does he do?
   h. Does he teach school?
   i. Does he load trucks?
   j. He looks strong.

4. Ask questions about Lucy and her father. Use **why is** or **why isn't**.
   a. Why isn't Lucy happy?
   b. Why is Lucy unhappy?
   c. Why isn't Lucy's father happy?
   d. Why is Lucy's father unhappy?
   e. Why isn't Lucy's father a teacher?
   f. Why is Lucy's father a painter?

5. Listen to these questions. Circle **yes** or **no**.
   a. Do Terry and Lucy live on the same street?
   b. Does Lucy look happy?
   c. Does Lucy's father feel happy?
   d. Does Lucy's father work?
   e. Does he get enough money?
   f. Does he teach?
   g. Does he load trucks?
   h. Does he paint houses?
   i. Does he like his work?

6. You will hear two statements. Write numbers to show the correct order.
   a. Terry sees Lucy.
      Terry talks to Lucy.
   b. Lucy says nothing is wrong.
      Lucy says she is not happy.
   c. Lucy's father has a bad job.
      Lucy's father is unhappy.

7. Listen to these sentences.
   - Lucy and Terry live on Pitcairn Drive.
   - Lucy lives on Pitcairn Drive.

   Look at the **s** in "Lucy lives on Pitcairn Drive." Listen to the statement. Then write a statement with Lucy's name. Use an **s**.
   a. Terry and Lucy see each other.
   b. Terry and Lucy talk.
   c. Lucy and her father look unhappy.
   d. Lucy and her father feel unhappy.
   e. Lucy and her father work too much.

8. Write what you know about Lucy, Terry, and Lucy's father.
   a. Lucy and Terry live on the same street.
   b. Terry talks to Lucy.
   c. Lucy doesn't look happy.
   d. Lucy doesn't feel happy.
   e. Lucy's father doesn't feel happy.
   f. He works too hard.
   g. He paints houses.
   h. He hates his job.

Lesson 4: You Always Look Tired *page 18*

Joelle and Nancy work in a restaurant after school. Joelle cooks and Nancy is the cashier. Who looks tired, and why?

Joelle: We're not too busy now. I want some soup.

Nancy: Good idea! I want something to eat, too. I feel like a salad.

Joelle: Do you have a lot of homework today?

Nancy: I *always* have a lot of homework. And my parents are away, so I have to take care of the house and my sisters.

Joelle: Oh, where are they?

Nancy: They are on a ship somewhere on the Nile. Even when they are home, I have to take care of the house and my sisters. My parents are *always* busy.

Joelle: And you always look tired.

Nancy: And *you* always tell me how tired I look!

1. a. What do you know about Joelle? Write what you hear.
    1. She works in a restaurant.
    2. She cooks in a restaurant.
    3. She goes to school.
    4. She wants some soup.
    5. She works with Nancy.
    6. She works after school.
    7. She says Nancy looks tired.

   b. What do you know about Nancy? Write what you hear.
    1. She works in a restaurant.
    2. She goes to school.
    3. She feels like a salad.
    4. She has a lot of homework.
    5. She takes care of the house.
    6. She looks tired.

   c. What do you know about the restaurant? Write what you hear.
    1. Joelle is the cook.
    2. Nancy is the cashier.
    3. They have soup.
    4. They have salad.
    5. They are not busy.

2. Listen to the questions. Underline the correct answer for each question.
    a. Who works in a restaurant?
    b. Who cooks in the restaurant?
    c. Who is the cashier?
    d. Who has a lot of homework?
    e. Who is away?
    f. Who is on a ship?
    g. Who has to take care of the house?
    h. Who always looks tired?

3. Look at these words. Listen to the sentences. Put the correct word on each line.
    a. They work in a restaurant.
    b. Joelle cooks.
    c. Nancy is the cashier.
    d. They are not too busy.
    e. Joelle wants some soup.
    f. Nancy feels like a salad.
    g. She has a lot of homework.
    h. Her parents are away.
    i. She takes care of the house.
    j. She has two sisters.
    k. They are on a ship.
    l. The ship is on the Nile.
    m. They are always busy.
    n. She looks tired.

4. Ask questions about Nancy. Start your questions with **does**.
    a. Does she work?
    b. Does she want to eat?
    c. Does she have a lot of homework?
    d. Does she take care of the house?
    e. Does she have sisters?
    f. Does she look tired?

5. Listen to these questions. Circle **yes** or **no**.
    a. Does Joelle work?
    b. Does Joelle want to eat?
    c. Does Joelle work with Nancy?
    d. Does Joelle look tired?
    e. Does Joelle want a salad?
    f. Does Nancy have a lot of homework?
    g. Do Nancy's parents go away?
    h. Does Nancy have brothers?
    i. Does Nancy look tired?

6. You will hear two statements. Write numbers to show the correct order.
    a. They are not busy.
       They have something to eat.
    b. They go to school.
       They go to work.
    c. They work.
       They do their homework.
    d. Joelle says she wants some soup.
       Nancy says she wants a salad.
    e. Nancy says she wants a salad.
       Nancy says her parents are away.
    f. Joelle asks about homework.
       Joelle asks about Nancy's parents.
    g. Nancy says her parents are always busy.
       Joelle says Nancy looks tired.

7. Listen to these sentences.
   - Nancy works in a restaurant.
   - Do you work in a restaurant?

   Listen to the statement. Then write a question with **do you**.
   a. Nancy feels like a salad.
   b. Joelle cooks.
   c. Nancy looks tired.
   d. Joelle wants some soup.
   e. Nancy gets a lot of homework.
   f. Nancy takes care of the house.

8. Write what you know about Nancy.
   a. She works in a restaurant.
   b. She is a cashier.
   c. She wants a salad.
   d. She has a lot of homework.
   e. She takes care of the house.
   f. She has sisters.
   g. She looks tired.
   h. Her parents are away.
   i. They are on a ship.
   j. They are on the Nile.
   k. They are always busy.

Lesson 5: They Don't Even Have a Movie Theater *page 23*

Eva and Sylvia are friends. They sit next to each other in math class. They don't have any work to do now, and they are talking quietly. What news does Eva have?

Eva: Sylvia! We're moving.

Sylvia: What? Are you kidding?

Eva: No, I'm not kidding. We're moving soon.

Sylvia: When?

Eva: Next month.

Sylvia: Why?

Eva: My mom's job.

Sylvia: Where?

Eva: Outer Creek.

Sylvia: Outer Creek! It is a nice area, isn't it?

Eva: Sure. But I don't want to move. I like it right here in Franklin.

Sylvia: What's wrong with Outer Creek? They have lakes and lots of tennis courts, don't they?

Eva: Yes, and three fast-food restaurants. That's it. No soccer club, no shopping malls, no library. There is *nothing* downtown, just a train station and a newspaper store. They don't even have a movie theater!

Teacher *(in background)*: Shhh! Quiet over there!

1. a. What do you know about Eva? Write what you hear.
   1. She is moving.
   2. She likes Franklin.
   3. She plays soccer.
   4. She likes to shop.
   5. She likes to read.
   6. She likes the movies.

   b. What do you know about Outer Creek? Write what you hear.
   1. It is nice.
   2. There are lakes.
   3. There are tennis courts.
   4. There are three fast-food restaurants.
   5. There is a train station.
   6. There is a newspaper store.
   7. There is no library.
   8. There is nothing downtown.
   9. There is no soccer club.
   10. There are no shopping malls.
   11. There is no movie theater.

2. Listen to the questions. Underline the correct answer for each question.
   a. Where is Eva going?
   b. Where does Sylvia live?
   c. Where is Eva's mother's new job?
   d. Where can we get a quick meal?
   e. Where can we buy books and clothes?
   f. Where can we go to borrow a book?
   g. Where can we play soccer?
   h. Where can we get the paper?

3. Look at these words. Listen to the sentences. Put the correct word on each line.
   a. They are friends.
   b. She sits next to her.
   c. They don't have any work now.
   d. She is talking.
   e. Does she have some news?
   f. They are moving.
   g. She doesn't want to move.
   h. She likes it in Franklin.
   i. It is a nice area, isn't it?
   j. It has lakes.
   k. They don't have a movie theater, do they?

4. Outer Creek has different attractions than Franklin. Ask if it has these things.
   a. Are there lakes?
   b. Are there tennis courts?
   c. Are there three fast-food restaurants?
   d. Is there a soccer club?
   e. Are there any shopping malls?
   f. Is there a library?
   g. Is there a train station?
   h. Is there a newspaper store?
   i. Is there a movie theater?

5. Listen to these questions. Circle **yes** or **no**.
   a. Does Outer Creek have any lakes?
   b. Does it have tennis courts?
   c. Does it have fast-food restaurants?
   d. Does it have a soccer club?
   e. Does it have shopping malls?
   f. Does it have a library?
   g. Does it have a train station?
   h. Does it have a newspaper store?
   i. Does it have a movie theater?

6. You will hear two statements. Write numbers to show the correct order.
   a. Eva lives in Franklin.
      Eva lives in Outer Creek.
   b. Sylvia goes to math class.
      Sylvia talks to Eva.
   c. Sylvia talks to Eva.
      The teacher tells the girls to be quiet.
   d. Eva tells Sylvia she is moving.
      The teacher tells the girls to be quiet.
   e. Eva lives in Franklin.
      Eva's mother's job changes.

7. Listen to this question and answer.
   - Outer Creek has lakes, doesn't it?
   - Yes, it does.

   Listen to the question about Outer Creek. Then answer "Yes, it does" or "No, it doesn't."
   a. It has lakes, doesn't it?
   b. It has tennis courts, doesn't it?
   c. It has fast-food restaurants, doesn't it?
   d. It has a soccer club, doesn't it?
   e. It has shopping malls, doesn't it?
   f. It has a library, doesn't it?
   g. It has a train station, doesn't it?
   h. It has a newspaper store, doesn't it?
   i. It has a movie theater, doesn't it?

8. Write what you know about Sylvia, Eva, and Outer Creek.
    a. Sylvia and Eva are in math class.
    b. Sylvia sits next to Eva.
    c. Sylvia doesn't have any work now.
    d. Sylvia and Eva are talking.
    e. Eva has some news.
    f. Eva is moving.
    g. Eva's mother's job is changing.
    h. Eva doesn't want to move.
    i. Eva likes Franklin.

Lesson 6: Anything Else? *page 28*

Larry is getting ready for school. His uncle Bob is helping him. Does Larry like Bob to help him?

Bob: Larry, tuck in your shirt.
Larry: It is okay like this.
Bob: No, it isn't. Tuck it in. And comb your hair.
Larry: It's combed.
Bob: Are you wearing brown shoes and blue socks?
Larry: Sure am.
Bob: Put on your sneakers. They go better.
Larry: It doesn't matter.
Bob: Yes, it does.
Larry: I'm only going to school.
Bob: Change those shoes and your belt, and don't forget to comb your hair.
Larry: Anything else?

1. a. What do you know about Larry? Write what you hear.
    1. He is going to school.
    2. He is wearing a shirt and pants.
    3. He is wearing shoes and socks.
    4. He has an uncle.
    5. His uncle is helping him.

   b. What do you know about Uncle Bob? Write what you hear.
    1. He is helping Larry.
    2. He wants Larry to tuck in his shirt.
    3. He wants Larry to comb his hair.
    4. He wants Larry to put on his sneakers.

2. Listen to the questions. Underline the correct answer for each question.
    a. Who is the uncle?
    b. Who goes to school?
    c. What does his uncle want Larry to do with his shirt?
    d. What does his uncle want Larry to do with his hair?
    e. What does his uncle want Larry to do with his shoes?
    f. Why does his uncle want Larry to put on his sneakers?

3. Look at these words. Listen to the sentences. Put the correct word on each line.
   a. Larry, tuck in your shirt.
   b. No, it isn't.
   c. Comb your hair.
   d. Don't you have a blue shirt?
   e. Put on your sneakers.
   f. It goes better.
   g. It doesn't matter.
   h. Yes, it does.
   i. He is going to school.
   j. Don't forget your shoes.

4. Bob thinks Larry should do many things before he goes to school. Ask what is wrong with these things.
   a. What is wrong with his shirt?
   b. What is wrong with his hair?
   c. What is wrong with his shoes?
   d. What is wrong with his socks?
   e. What is wrong with his pants?
   f. What is wrong with his belt?

5. Listen to these questions. Circle **yes** or **no**.
   a. Is Larry getting ready for school?
   b. Is he helping his uncle?
   c. Are his shoes brown?
   d. Are his socks brown?
   e. Does his hair look combed?
   f. Does Larry like Bob to help him?

6. You will hear two statements. Write numbers to show the correct order.
   a. Larry and Bob are talking.
      Larry goes to school.
   b. Larry puts on his shirt.
      Larry goes to school.
   c. Larry puts on his socks.
      Larry puts on his shoes.
   d. Larry combs his hair.
      Larry combs his hair again.
   e. Larry puts on his pants.
      Larry puts on his belt.

7. Listen to these sentences.
   • Put on your brown socks.
   • Don't put on your blue socks.
   Listen to the sentence. Then write a sentence with the color blue. Use **don't**.
   a. Put on your white sneakers.
   b. Put on your yellow shirt.
   c. Put on your red blouse.
   d. Put on your orange tie.
   e. Put on your black shoes.
   f. Put on your gray pants.
   g. Put on your red boots.

8. Write what you know about Larry.
    a. He goes to school.
    b. He has an uncle.
    c. His uncle's name is Bob.
    d. Bob is his uncle.
    e. His shirt is out.
    f. His hair doesn't look combed.
    g. He is wearing brown shoes.
    h. He is wearing blue socks.
    i. He is not wearing sneakers.

Lesson 7: Can You Draw a Stegosaurus? *page 32*

Victor is drawing pictures for a children's book. He is sitting at the kitchen table with his aunt Charlotte. What illustration is giving him problems?

Victor: This iced tea is great! What is in it?

Charlotte: Tea and water. How is it going?

Victor: Not so great. I have a good brontosaurus and a good tyrannosaurus, but this stegosaurus is coming out all wrong. Can you draw a stegosaurus?

Charlotte: I can't draw a stick figure. Those spikes do look strange.

Victor: They are too thick, aren't they?

Charlotte: Yes, and that head is too big for the body. A stegosaurus has a tiny head, doesn't it? And your stegosaurus's legs are too long, don't you think?

Victor: That's right! For someone who can't draw a stick figure, you know a lot about art!

1. a. What do you know about Victor? Write what you hear.
    1. He is drinking iced tea.
    2. He is drawing pictures.
    3. He is sitting in the kitchen.
    4. His aunt's name is Charlotte.
    5. He is having problems with the stegosaurus.
   b. What do you know about Charlotte? Write what you hear.
    1. She is sitting in the kitchen.
    2. She cannot draw a stick figure.
    3. She knows a lot about art.
    4. She knows how to make iced tea.
    5. She is helping Victor.
   c. What do you know about stegosauruses? Write what you hear.
    1. They have small heads.
    2. They have spikes.
    3. They have short legs.

2. Listen to the questions. Underline the correct answer for each question.
    a. Why is Victor drawing pictures?
    b. What pictures does he like?
    c. What is in the iced tea?
    d. What is wrong with the stegosaurus's spikes?
    e. What is wrong with the head?
    f. What is wrong with the legs?
    g. What can Charlotte draw?

3. Look at these words. Listen to the sentences. Put the correct word on each line.
    a. Victor is drawing pictures.
    b. He is sitting in the kitchen.
    c. What is giving him problems?
    d. I have a good brontosaurus.
    e. This dinosaur is coming out wrong.
    f. I can't draw a dinosaur.
    g. That dinosaur does look strange.
    h. Those legs do look bad.
    i. They are too thick, aren't they?
    j. They look too thick, don't they?
    k. It looks too big, doesn't it?

4. Victor is having some problems. Ask if he is having a problem with these things.
    a. Is he having a problem with the iced tea?
    b. Is he having a problem with his aunt?
    c. Is he having a problem with the dinosaurs?
    d. Is he having a problem with the brontosaurus?
    e. Is he having a problem with the tyrannosaurus?
    f. Is he having a problem with the stegosaurus?
    g. Is he having a problem with the spikes?
    h. Is he having a problem with the legs?
    i. Is he having a problem with the head?

5. Listen to these questions. Circle **yes** or **no**.
    a. Can Charlotte draw well?
    b. Can Victor draw well?
    c. Are Charlotte and Victor in the tea room?
    d. Is Victor drinking iced tea?
    e. Can Charlotte draw a stegosaurus?
    f. Can Victor draw a brontosaurus?
    g. Does a stegosaurus have a big head?
    h. Does it have spikes?

6. You will hear two statements. Write numbers to show the correct order.
   a. Victor draws a brontosaurus.
      Victor draws a stegosaurus.
   b. Someone makes iced tea.
      Victor drinks iced tea.
   c. Victor draws a tyrannosaurus.
      Victor draws a stegosaurus.
   d. Charlotte says the spikes look strange.
      She says the head is too big.
   e. Charlotte says she can't draw.
      Victor says Charlotte knows a lot about art.

7. Listen to these sentences.
   - A stegosaurus always gives him problems.
   - What **is** giv**ing** him problems **now**?

   Look at the **s** in the statement. Look at the **is, –ing**, and **now** in the question.
   Listen to the statement. Then complete the question.
   a. His aunt always helps him.
   b. His aunt always gives him iced tea.
   c. Victor always drinks iced tea.
   d. Victor always draws dinosaurs.
   e. The stegosaurus always comes out wrong.

8. Write what you know about Victor, Charlotte, and stegosauruses.
   a. Victor is drawing pictures.
   b. Charlotte is Victor's aunt.
   c. Charlotte cannot draw well.
   d. Victor draws well.
   e. Victor is drawing a stegosaurus now.
   f. He is having problems.
   g. A stegosaurus has a small head.
   h. It has spikes.
   i. It has short legs.

Lesson 8: Does the Sun Ever Come Out in Bergen? *page 37*

Willie, Maria, and their daughter Pilar are in a hotel in Bergen, Norway. Where does Pilar go, and what does she learn?

Willie: Wake up, Maria. Today is our last day in Bergen.

Maria: Is the sun out?

Willie: No. It is raining.

Maria: Again? This makes three days in Bergen and three days without sun. Where's Pilar?

Willie: Out for a walk. *(sound of key in door and door opening)* Here she is.

Pilar: I'm back. Rain again. *(sound of door closing)*

Maria: Bad luck.

Pilar: Not really. The man who works at the front desk says it always rains in Bergen.

Maria: Does the sun ever come out?

Pilar: He says there is an old joke in Bergen. A tourist meets a child on the street. It is raining. They talk about the weather. The tourist asks, "Does the sun ever come out in Bergen?" The boy answers, "I don't know, I am only eight years old."

1. a. What do you know about Willie? Write what you hear.
   1. He is in Bergen, Norway.
   2. He is Pilar's father.
   3. He is Maria's husband.

   b. What do you know about Pilar? Write what you hear.
   1. She is in Bergen, Norway.
   2. She is Maria's daughter.
   3. She goes for a walk.
   4. She talks to the man at the front desk.

2. Listen to the questions. Underline the correct answer for each question.
   a. Who is Pilar's father?
   b. What is the weather like?
   c. For how many days is this family in Bergen?
   d. Whom does Pilar talk to?
   e. Where is the family?
   f. Who talks at the front desk?
   g. Who talks on the street?

3. Look at these words. Listen to the sentences. Put the correct word on each line.
   a. Today is our last day here.
   b. It is raining.
   c. The man says it always rains.
   d. Does the sun come out?
   e. A tourist meets a child.
   f. They talk about the weather.
   g. She asks, "Where is the sun?"
   h. He answers, "I don't know."

4. Ask who says these things in the conversation.
   a. Who says it is time for Maria to wake up?
   b. Who says it is raining?
   c. Who says Pilar is out for a walk?
   d. Who says it always rains?
   e. Who says there is an old joke?
   f. Who says he doesn't know?
   g. Who says he is eight years old?

5. Listen to these questions. Circle **yes** or **no**.
   a. Is Maria in Norway?
   b. Is Pilar in Bergen?
   c. Is it sunny?
   d. Is Pilar the daughter?
   e. Is Willie the son?
   f. Is the boy in the joke eight years old?
   g. Is Pilar with her mother and father?

6. You will hear two statements. Write numbers to show the correct order.
   a. Pilar is out for a walk.
      Pilar is back.
   b. Maria is sleeping.
      Maria wakes up.
   c. Pilar talks to the man at the front desk.
      Pilar goes back to the room.
   d. Willie wakes up.
      Willie sees the rain.
   e. The tourist comes to Bergen.
      The tourist meets a child on the street.
   f. The man at the front desk tells Pilar a joke.
      Pilar tells Willie and Maria a joke.

7. Listen to these sentences.
   - Willie tells Maria to wake up.
   - **Does** Willie **tell** Maria to wake up?
   Look at the s in "Willie tells Maria to wake up." Look at **Does** and **tell** in the question. Listen to the statement. Then write a question with **Does**.
   a. Maria asks if the sun is out.
   b. Willie tells Maria it is raining.
   c. Maria asks where Pilar is.
   d. Willie says she is back.
   e. Pilar says it is raining again.
   f. The man at the front desk says it always rains.
   g. He says there is an old joke.
   h. The tourist asks if the sun comes out.
   i. The boy says he is only eight.

8. Write what you know about Willie, Maria, Pilar, and Bergen.
   a. Willie is waking Maria.
   b. Pilar is out for a walk.
   c. Maria doesn't like rain.
   d. A man is working at the front desk.
   e. He is telling a joke.
   f. It always rains in Bergen.
   g. The sun never comes out in Bergen.
   h. The tourist asks a question.
   i. The boy says he is eight.

Lesson 9: I Am Not Cut Out for Parachuting *page 42*

Every Saturday Jane and her brother Gary jump from airplanes. Daniel and Gary are good friends. Does Daniel want to go with them?

Jane: Hi, Daniel.

Daniel: Hi, Jane. How is Gary?

Jane: He is over his cold and he is feeling fine.

Daniel: So it is back to the skies tomorrow, huh?

Jane: That's right. Why don't you come with us?

Daniel: I like watching from the ground.

Jane: It is a lot of fun.

Daniel: What time are you going?

Jane: I don't know yet. Gary has to work in the morning. I guess around two o'clock. Come with us this time.

Daniel: No, thanks. I'm not cut out for parachuting.

1. a. What do you know about Gary? Write what you hear.
    1. He is Jane's brother.
    2. He is over his cold.
    3. He is feeling fine.
    4. He is going parachuting.
    5. He is working.

   b. What do you know about Daniel? Write what you hear.
    1. He is Gary's friend.
    2. He likes to watch.
    3. He is talking to Jane.
    4. He is not cut out for parachuting.

   c. What do you know about Jane? Write what you hear.
    1. She is Gary's sister.
    2. She is talking to Daniel.
    3. She asks Daniel to go.
    4. She likes to parachute.

2. Listen to the questions. Underline the correct answer for each question.
   a. Who is Daniel?
   b. Who is over a cold?
   c. Who is going parachuting?
   d. When are they going?
   e. What time do they go?
   f. Who does Jane ask to go?
   g. Why doesn't Daniel go?
   h. What does Daniel do when Jane and Gary are parachuting?

3. Look at these words. Listen to the sentences. Put the correct word on each line.
   a. He is feeling fine now.
   b. Why don't you come?
   c. I like watching.
   d. What time are you going?
   e. I don't know yet.
   f. He has to work.
   g. I guess around 2:00.
   h. Come with us.
   i. I don't like parachuting.

4. Daniel doesn't like parachuting. Ask why not. Then ask more questions with **why not**.
   a. Why doesn't Daniel like parachuting?
   b. Why doesn't Daniel like high places?
   c. Why doesn't Daniel like flying?
   d. Why doesn't Gary like being sick?
   e. Why doesn't Gary like working?
   f. Why doesn't Gary like being at home?
   g. Why doesn't Jane like working?
   h. Why doesn't Jane like being on the ground?
   i. Why doesn't Jane like watching?

5. Listen to these questions. Circle **yes** or **no**.
   a. Is Gary Jane's brother?
   b. Does Daniel jump from airplanes?
   c. Is Gary over his cold?
   d. Is he feeling fine?
   e. Does Daniel like parachuting?
   f. Is Jane cut out for parachuting?
   g. Does Gary work in the morning?
   h. Are they going in the morning?

6. You will hear two statements. Write numbers to show the correct order.
   a. Gary is sick.
      Gary is fine.
   b. Gary goes parachuting.
      Gary comes back.
   c. Gary works.
      Gary goes parachuting.
   d. Jane and Daniel talk.
      Jane and Gary go parachuting.
   e. Jane asks Daniel to go parachuting.
      Daniel says, "No, thanks."

7. Listen to these sentences.
   - Gary has to work in the morning.
   - Gary works in the morning.

   Look at the **s** in "works." Listen to the statement. Then write a statement with **s**.
   a. Daniel has to talk to Jane.
   b. Gary has to feel fine.
   c. Jane has to parachute.
   d. Daniel has to stay on the ground.
   e. Gary has to jump at two.

8. Write what you know about Jane, Gary, and Daniel.
   a. Jane is going parachuting.
   b. Gary is going parachuting.
   c. Daniel is not going parachuting.
   d. Daniel likes watching from the ground.
   e. Daniel doesn't jump from airplanes.
   f. Gary has to work.

Lesson 10: Call Back Later *page 47*

Bill Mason calls Mario. Does he talk to him?

(sound of phone ringing)

Woman: Hello.
Bill: Hi, this is Bill Mason. Is Mario there?
Woman: No, Bill. He is at baseball practice.
Bill: When does he get home?
Woman: When? Six o'clock. Call him after dinner, at seven.
Bill: I have my piano lesson at seven. How about eight?
Woman: Eight o'clock is fine.
Bill: Thanks. Good-bye.
Woman: Good-bye.

1. a. What do you know about Mario? Write what you hear.
   1. He lives with his mother.
   2. He is at baseball practice.
   3. He gets home at 6:00.
   4. He eats dinner at 6:30.

   b. What do you know about Bill? Write what you hear.
   1. He is not at Mario's house.
   2. He calls Mario.
   3. He is not at baseball practice.
   4. He takes piano lessons.
   5. He is going to call back at 8:00.

2. Listen to the questions. Underline the correct answer for each question.
    a. What is Bill's last name?
    b. Is Mario at baseball practice?
    c. What time does Mario get home?
    d. What time does Bill have his piano lesson?
    e. What time can Bill call Mario?
    f. Where is Mario?
    g. What does Bill have at seven?

3. Look at these words. Listen to the sentences. Put the correct word on each line.
    a. This is Bill Mason.
    b. Is Mario there?
    c. He is at baseball practice.
    d. When does he get back?
    e. Call him after dinner.
    f. I have a piano lesson.
    g. Eight o'clock is fine.

4. Ask questions with **when**.
    a. When does Mario have baseball practice?
    b. When does Mario get home?
    c. When does Bill call Mario?
    d. When does Mario have dinner?
    e. When does Bill have dinner?
    f. When does Bill have a piano lesson?
    g. When does Bill talk to Mario?

5. Listen to these questions. Circle **yes** or **no**.
    a. Is Mario calling Bill?
    b. Is Mario playing baseball?
    c. Does Mario get home at six o'clock?
    d. Does Bill take piano lessons?
    e. Is the piano lesson at six o'clock?

6. You will hear two statements. Write numbers to show the correct order.
    a. Mario goes to baseball practice.
       Bill calls Mario.
    b. Bill calls Mario.
       Bill talks to Mario's mother.
    c. Mario goes to baseball practice.
       Mario has dinner.
    d. Bill has dinner.
       Bill has a piano lesson.
    e. Mario has dinner.
       Bill has a piano lesson.
    f. Mario has baseball practice.
       Bill has a piano lesson.

7. Listen to this question and answer.
   - Does Mario have baseball practice every day?
   - No, he has it every Tuesday.

   Listen to the question. Write the answer, using **every Tuesday**.
   a. Does Bill play soccer every day?
   b. Does Bill have his piano lesson every day?
   c. Does Mario go to karate class every day?
   d. Does Bill have his ski lesson every day?
   e. Does Mario have his stamp club meeting every day?
   f. Do Bill and Mario play tennis every day?
   g. Do Bill and Mario have basketball practice every day?

8. Write what you know about Bill and Mario.
   a. Mario is not at home.
   b. Mario is at baseball practice.
   c. Mario gets home at 6:00.
   d. Mario eats dinner at 6:30.
   e. Bill is calling Mario.
   f. Bill is talking to Mario's mother.
   g. Bill takes piano lessons.
   h. Bill's piano lesson is at 7:00.

Unit 2

Lesson 11: I Ate Too Much Pizza *page 55*

Li Za and Jenny are friends. They are at the beach. What time of day is it?

Li Za: Did you hear that rain last night, Jenny?

Jenny: It was awful. And it was raining this morning when I got up.

Li Za: Where did you go for breakfast?

Jenny: Nowhere. I had breakfast at home with my aunt and my cousins. We all went out for pizza at noon. Then I came here.

Li Za: How long are your visitors staying?

Jenny: When it started raining yesterday, they wanted to leave. But when they saw the sun come out, they decided to stay two more days.

Li Za: Let's go into the water.

Jenny: Go ahead. My stomach doesn't feel very good. I think I ate too much pizza.

1. Listen to the question and answer. Write the question.
    a. Did it rain?
       Yes, it did.
    b. Did Jenny go out for breakfast?
       No, she didn't.
    c. Did she eat breakfast at home?
       Yes, she did.
    d. Did her aunt have breakfast with her?
       Yes, she did.
    e. Did they go out for pizza?
       Yes, they did.
    f. Did Jenny eat too much pizza?
       Yes, she did.

2. Listen to the questions. Circle **yes** or **no**.
    a. Did Jenny hear the rain?
    b. Did Li Za hear the rain?
    c. Did it rain last night?
    d. Did it rain this morning?
    e. Did Jenny go out for breakfast?
    f. Did Jenny go out for lunch?
    g. Did Jenny have pizza at noon?
    h. Did Jenny go to the beach before lunch?
    i. Did Jenny's visitors want to leave yesterday?
    j. Did the sun come out?
    k. Did Jenny eat too much?

3. Listen to the questions. Complete the answers.
   a. Did it rain last night?
   b. Did it snow last night?
   c. Did Jenny hear the rain?
   d. Did Li Za hear the rain?
   e. Did Jenny's aunt come to visit?
   f. Did Jenny's cousins come to visit?
   g. Did it start to rain yesterday?
   h. Did the sun come out?

4. Listen to these answers. Which question goes with each answer? Draw a circle around the number of the correct question.
   a. Yes, it rained all day.
   b. Yes, it rained all night.
   c. No, it rained.
   d. Yes, she got up at 7:00.
   e. No, she didn't feel like swimming.
   f. No, she went out for lunch.
   g. Yes, they came to visit.
   h. Yes, it came out at noon.

5. Listen to these sentences.
   - It rained.
   - It rained, didn't it?

   Now listen to each statement and complete the question.
   a. Jenny ate pizza.
   b. Jenny ate at home.
   c. Jenny's cousins had breakfast at home.
   d. Jenny came to the beach.
   e. It started raining.
   f. The sun came out.
   g. They went to the beach.
   h. She ate too much pizza.

6. Listen to these questions. For each question, circle the number of the correct answer.
   a. Did it rain last night?
   b. Did Li Za go with Jenny for pizza?
   c. Did Jenny have pizza for breakfast?
   d. Did the visitors decide to stay?
   e. Did the sun come out?
   f. Did Li Za eat too much?
   g. Did they go to the beach in the sun?

Now stop the tape and do exercise 7 in your book.

Lesson 12: I Got a Cordless Phone for $6.99! *page 59*

Roberta and Walter are sister and brother. It is Saturday morning, and Walter just came into the house. Did he buy something good?

Roberta: Where were you?

Walter: At Gil's Give-Away. They are having a sale.

Roberta: I know. Suzie told me and I read about it in the paper. What did you get?

Walter: I got a cordless phone for $6.99.

Roberta: Walter, again? You got a phone on sale there before. It cost $3.99. It had a cord. It came in eight different colors. It was the newest model. It had no guarantee, and it lasted four days.

Walter: I know. That was a mistake. But this phone is beautiful. I left it in the car. Let me get it.

Roberta: Don't bother. You can't get a cordless phone for $7.00.

1. Listen to the question and answer. Write the question.
    a. Who went to the store?
       Walter did.
    b. Who just came home?
       Walter did.
    c. Who told Roberta about the sale?
       Suzie did.
    d. Who read about it?
       Roberta did.
    e. Who got a phone?
       Walter did.
    f. Who bought a phone before?
       Walter did.
    g. Who made a mistake?
       Walter did.
    h. Who left the phone in the car?
       Walter did.

2. Listen to the questions. Circle **yes** or **no**.
    a. Did Walter go to Gil's Give-Away?
    b. Did he buy a cordless phone?
    c. Did it cost $3.99?
    d. Did Walter tell Suzie about the phone?
    e. Did Walter buy a bad phone once?
    f. Did it have a guarantee?
    g. Did it last long?

3. Listen to the questions. Write the answers.
   a. Who just came home?
   b. Who went to Gil's?
   c. Who bought a cordless phone?
   d. Who told Roberta about the sale first?
   e. Who read about the sale?
   f. Who made a mistake once at Gil's?
   g. Who got mad?
   h. Who left the new phone in the car?

4. Listen to these answers. Which question goes with each answer? Draw a circle around the number of the correct question.
   a. Walter went.
   b. Yes, he bought one for $6.99.
   c. Suzie told her.
   d. Yes, she read about it in the paper.
   e. Walter got one.
   f. Walter did.
   g. Yes, she got very mad.
   h. Walter made a mistake.

5. Listen to these sentences.
   - Who bought a phone?
   - Roberta didn't buy one, did she?
   - No, she didn't.

   Now listen to each question. Complete the second question and the answer.
   a. Who went to Gil's?
   b. Who bought a phone?
   c. Who told Roberta?
   d. Who got a phone for $3.99?
   e. Who read about it in the paper?
   f. Who got a phone with no guarantee?
   g. Who made a mistake?
   h. Who left the phone in the car?

6. Listen to these questions. For each question, circle the number of the correct answer.
   a. Who went to Gil's?
   b. Did Roberta buy a phone?
   c. Who read about the sale?
   d. Did the phone cost $6.99?
   e. Who told Roberta about the sale first?
   f. Did the $3.99 phone last four weeks?
   g. Who made a mistake?
   h. Did Roberta leave the phone in the car?

Now stop the tape and do exercise 7 in your book.

Lesson 13: Where Did You Buy Your Down Jacket? *page 64*

Ilyan and Omar are friends. It is winter, and they are ice-skating on a lake. Where did Ilyan get his jacket?

Ilyan: This ice is too choppy!

Omar: They had a hockey game this morning. Great Gulch won.

Ilyan: December and January were sure warm, weren't they?

Omar: Yes. I took out my winter jacket for the first time during the ice storm last week. Yours is down, isn't it?

Ilyan: One hundred percent.

Omar: Where did you get it?

Ilyan: From a catalog. It was the first time I ever tried to get something from a catalog. And the last time, too. "The Down Place," it's called, and it took three tries. They kept sending me the wrong thing.

Omar: No kidding.

Ilyan: First I saw this great sale: $95, sixteen colors. I sent away for a large, in blue. Two weeks later a small came. I sent it back.

Omar: Who paid?

Ilyan: They did. Next I got a large, but it was green. So I sent that one back, too. Finally, they sent me what I asked for. It took two months.

1. Listen to the question and answer. Write the question.
    a. What did they have?
       A hockey game.
    b. Who won?
       Great Gulch.
    c. Was December warm?
       Yes, it was.
    d. Was January warm?
       Yes, it was.
    e. When was the ice storm?
       Last week.
    f. Who saw a sale?
       Ilyan did.

2. Listen to the questions. Circle **yes** or **no**.
    a. Is the ice smooth?
    b. Is Ilyan's jacket down?
    c. Is Ilyan's jacket from "The Down Place"?
    d. Did it cost $9.99?
    e. Did he send away for a small jacket?
    f. Did they have sixteen colors?
    g. Did he want a blue jacket?
    h. Did he get his jacket in two days?

3. Listen to the questions. Complete the answers.
   a. What is the ice like?
   b. What was December like?
   c. What was January like?
   d. What was last week like?
   e. What is Ilyan's jacket like?
   f. What color is it?
   g. What size is it?

4. Listen to these answers. Which question goes with each answer? Draw a circle around the number of the correct question.
   a. It's choppy.
   b. Great Gulch won.
   c. The ice storm was last week.
   d. He got it from a catalog.
   e. It's called "The Down Place."
   f. It cost $95.
   g. He wears a large.
   h. He sent for blue.
   i. It took two months.

5. Listen to these sentences.
   - They are skating now.
   - Yes they are, and they skated before.

   Now listen to each sentence and complete the second sentence.
   a. Great Gulch is winning now.
   b. Omar is wearing his jacket now.
   c. Ilyan is wearing a down jacket now.
   d. He is ordering from a catalog now.
   e. He is looking at a sale.
   f. He is talking about a jacket now.
   g. They are looking at a catalog.
   h. They are sending away for jackets.

6. Listen to these questions. For each question, circle the number of the correct answer.
   a. What is the ice like?
   b. Who won the hockey game?
   c. What were December and January like?
   d. When did Omar take out his jacket?
   e. When was the ice storm?
   f. How much of Ilyan's jacket is down?
   g. Where did Ilyan get his jacket?
   h. How much did it cost?
   i. How many colors did it come in?
   j. What is Ilyan's jacket like?
   k. Who paid to send the jacket back?

Now stop the tape and do exercise 7 in your book.

Lesson 14: How Did You Break Your Elbow? *page 69*

Nancy and Bob work in a drugstore after school. It is 3:30, and they are both walking in.

Nancy: Hi, Bob!

Bob: I heard. I was talking to your brother Robert at hockey practice last night. How did you break your elbow?

Nancy: I fell during hockey practice the night before last.

Bob: How did you fall?

Nancy: At the beginning of practice, Winnie fell right in front of me. I jumped over her. Michelle smashed into me and knocked me down.

Bob: That was some practice!

Nancy: Oh, no. I was fine. I got right up, but Lynne skated into me. I fell on my elbow.

Bob: What then?

Nancy: I sat on the bench from 5:00 to 5:30. Then I decided not to play anymore. I called Robert and he came for me at 6:00. We got some Chinese food at Lucky Star, and then we went home. I couldn't move my arm, so Mom took me to the hospital at 7:30.

Bob: I broke my wrist once playing volleyball. I was at summer camp. I didn't know the other kids. We got into teams. The girl across the net from me was a state champion. I didn't see her return the ball. I was just happy it got my wrist, and not my head!

1. Listen to the question and answer. Write the question.
    a. Who is Nancy's brother?
       Robert is Nancy's brother.
    b. Where was Bob last night?
       At hockey practice.
    c. What did Nancy break?
       She broke her elbow.
    d. Who fell in front of Nancy?
       Winnie fell in front of Nancy.
    e. Who smashed into Nancy?
       Michelle smashed into Nancy.
    f. Who skated into Nancy?
       Lynne skated into Nancy.
    g. Did Nancy sit on the bench?
       Yes, she did.
    h. Whom did Nancy call?
       She called Robert.
    i. Who came for her?
       Robert came.
    j. Who took her to the hospital?
       Her mother took her.

2. Listen to the questions. Circle **yes** or **no**.
    a. Did Winnie fall in front of Nancy?
    b. Did Nancy fall on her?
    c. Did Nancy fall on her knee?
    d. Did Nancy call Bob?
    e. Did Robert and Nancy get some hamburgers?
    f. Did she go to the hospital?

g. Was Bob playing volleyball?
h. Was Bob at the beach?
i. Was the state champion a boy?
j. Did Bob break his wrist?

3. Listen to the questions. Complete the answers.
    a. Who played hockey last night?
    b. Who fell in front of Nancy?
    c. Who jumped over Winnie?
    d. Who smashed into Nancy?
    e. Who skated into Nancy?
    f. Who came for Nancy?
    g. Who took Nancy to the hospital?
    h. Who broke his wrist?

4. Listen to these answers. Which question goes with each answer? Draw a circle around the number of the correct question.
    a. He heard it at hockey practice.
    b. He heard that Nancy broke her elbow.
    c. She broke it the night before last.
    d. She broke it at hockey practice.
    e. She sat on the bench.
    f. She sat there from 5:00 to 5:30.
    g. Robert came for her.
    h. He came for her at 6:00.
    i. She couldn't move her arm.
    j. She took her to the hospital.

5. Listen to these sentences.
    • I didn't hear.
    • But I heard.
    Now listen to each sentence and complete the second sentence.
    a. I didn't talk.
    b. I didn't jump.
    c. I didn't get up.
    d. I didn't skate into her.
    e. I didn't fall.
    f. I didn't sit on the bench.
    g. I didn't decide to play.
    h. I didn't call Robert.
    i. I didn't come for her.
    j. I didn't get Chinese food.
    k. I didn't go home.
    l. I didn't move my arm.

6. Listen to these questions. For each question, circle the number of the correct answer.
    a. Who was talking to Robert?
    b. When did Nancy break her elbow?
    c. When did Winnie fall in front of Nancy?
    d. What did Michelle do?

e. What did Lynne do?
f. What did Nancy break?
g. Where did Nancy and Robert get dinner?
h. Where did Nancy's mother take her?

Now stop the tape and do exercise 7 in your book.

Lesson 15: This Soup Is Awful! Did You Forget the Salt? *page 74*

Gary and Joe are brothers. They made lunch. Joe made the salad, and Gary made the soup. Does it sound like a good meal?

Gary: Hey, Joe, that salad looks great! What did you put in it?

Joe: Just what you see. I took some of Dad's famous salad dressing, and I put in all the vegetables I could find. The carrots are from the garden. I got the cheese downtown, and the beans are out of a can. Please pass me a bowl of soup.

Gary: Here you go. Take some bread. Dorothy made it.

Joe: Dorothy? Who is Dorothy?

Gary: The woman across the street. She just baked it. It is still warm.

Joe: Arghh! This soup is awful! Did you forget the salt?

Gary: No. I never put salt in it.

Joe: Please pass the salt. It never tasted bad before.

Gary: With peppers, onions, and pasta, you don't need salt.

Joe: I do!

1. Listen to the question and answer. Write the question.
    a. Who made lunch?
       Gary and Joe did.
    b. Who made the salad?
       Joe did.
    c. Who made the salad dressing?
       Dad did.
    d. Who made the bread?
       Dorothy did.
    e. Who made the soup?
       Gary did.
    f. What did Joe make?
       He made the salad.
    g. What did Gary make?
       He made the soup.
    h. What did Dad make?
       He made the salad dressing.
    i. What did Dorothy make?
       She made the bread.
    j. What did Gary put in the soup?
       He put in peppers, onions, and pasta.
    k. What did Joe put in the salad?
       He put in vegetables and dressing.

2. Listen to the questions. Circle **yes** or **no**.
    a. Did they make lunch?
    b. Did Joe make the soup?
    c. Did the carrots come from the garden?

d. Did the cheese come from Dorothy?
   e. Did Joe get the beans from a can?
   f. Did Gary make the bread?
   g. Did Joe like the soup?
   h. Did Gary forget the salt?

3. Listen to the questions. Complete the answers.
   a. What did Joe and Gary make?
   b. What did Joe make?
   c. What did Gary make?
   d. What did their father make?
   e. What did Dorothy make?
   f. What did Joe put in the salad?

4. Listen to these answers. Which question goes with each answer? Draw a circle around the number of the correct question.
   a. He put in vegetables and salad dressing.
   b. The carrots did.
   c. The beans did.
   d. The cheese did.
   e. The bread did.
   f. Gary's soup.
   g. Peppers, onions, and pasta.

5. Listen to these sentences.
   - Gary made lunch.
   - What did he make?

   Now listen to each sentence. Then write a question with **What**.
   a. Gary and Joe made lunch.
   b. Joe made the salad.
   c. Gary made the soup.
   d. Dad made the salad dressing.
   e. They put vegetables in the salad.
   f. They used cheese in the salad.
   g. They added beans to the salad.
   h. They threw in some carrots.
   i. They had bread with lunch.
   j. Dorothy made the bread.

6. Listen to these questions. For each question, circle the number of the correct answer.
   a. Did Gary forget the salt?
   b. What didn't Joe like?
   c. What came from across the street?
   d. What was in the salad?
   e. What meal did Gary and Joe make?
   f. What carrots did Joe use?
   g. What cheese did he use?
   h. What beans did he use?

Now stop the tape and do exercise 7 in your book.

Unit 3

Lesson 16: I Won't Be Back until August *page 81*

Emma and Wendy meet in a supermarket. What plans does Wendy have for the summer?

Wendy: Hi, Emma!

Emma: Wendy!

Wendy: I'm glad to see you. I'm going away June 24, and I wanted to say good-bye.

Emma: Will you be back for the tennis games at the end of June?

Wendy: Not a chance.

Emma: How about the Fourth of July picnic?

Wendy: Uh-uh.

Emma: The swim meet the third week in July?

Wendy: No.

Emma: My birthday party July 25?

Wendy: No, Emma, I won't be back until August.

Emma: August? Where are you going?

Wendy: Up to Lake Michigan to sail for a week, then we are going to go camping in Oregon for a month. After that we are flying to New Orleans for my brother's wedding. We will stay there until the middle of August.

Emma: That sounds great! I have to go; my cousin is waiting outside. See you in August! Bye!

Wendy: Bye, Emma!

1. Listen to the questions. Circle **yes** or **no**.
    a. Is Wendy going to go away?
    b. Is Wendy going to go to the tennis games?
    c. Will Wendy be at the Fourth of July picnic?
    d. Will she go to the swim meet?
    e. Is she going to be at Emma's birthday party?
    f. Is she going to go sailing?
    g. Will she be going camping?
    h. Is she going to go to Oregon?
    i. Will she be in New Orleans?
    j. Is she going to see her brother?
    k. Will she back in August?

2. Listen to the questions. For each question, circle the number of the correct answer.
   a. Who is going to go away?
   b. When are the tennis games going to be?
   c. There is going to be a picnic, isn't there?
   d. What is going to happen the third week in July?
   e. When will Emma be having her birthday party?
   f. When is Wendy coming back?
   g. Who is going camping for a month?
   h. How is Wendy going to get to New Orleans?
   i. Where are Emma and Wendy talking?

Now stop the tape and do exercises 3 and 4 in your book.

5. Look at these sentences.
   - Did Wendy go away yesterday?
   - No, she is going away tomorrow.

   Listen to the question with **yesterday**. Then write the answer with **tomorrow**.
   a. Did Wendy say good-bye yesterday?
   b. Did she come back yesterday?
   c. Did she go to the swim meet yesterday?
   d. Did she go sailing yesterday?
   e. Did she go camping yesterday?
   f. Did she fly to New Orleans yesterday?
   g. Did she see her uncle yesterday?

6. Look at this question and answer.
   - Are you going away in June?
   - No, I won't go away until August.

   Listen to the questions and write the answers. Use **until August**.
   a. Are you playing tennis in June?
   b. Are you going swimming in June?
   c. Are you going sailing in June?
   d. Are you going to Oregon in June?

Lesson 17: You Don't Play Football! *page 85*

David and his mother are talking. What two things does David have to do before dinner?

David: Bye, Mom.
Mother: Where are you going?
David: I'm going to football practice.
Mother: You don't play football!
David: I'm going to take pictures of the team.
Mother: What time will you be back?
David: Before dinner.
Mother: I hope so! We are having fried chicken tonight. I want you to pick it up.
David: What time are we going to eat?
Mother: At six. I'll call and order it for five forty-five. Will you get it?
David: Where?
Mother: Bundy's.
David: Sure.
Mother: Do you have enough money?
David: Yes. I have fifteen dollars with me. It won't be more than that, will it?
Mother: No. It will probably be about twelve or thirteen.
David: See you later.
Mother: Don't forget to pick up dinner!

1. Listen to the questions. Circle **yes** or **no**.
    a. Is David going to football practice?
    b. Is he going to play football?
    c. Is he going to take pictures?
    d. Is he going home for dinner?
    e. Is he going to get the chicken?
    f. Are they going to eat pizza?
    g. Will dinner cost about $5.45?
    h. Is he getting dinner at Bundy's?
    i. Will dinner be more than $15.00?

2. Listen to the questions. For each question, circle the number of the correct answer.
    a. Where is David going?
    b. What is David going to do at football practice?
    c. When is David getting home?
    d. When is David stopping for dinner?
    e. When will David's mother call to order the chicken?
    f. When will David pay for dinner?
    g. When will David see his mother again?
    h. When will David and his family have dinner?

Now stop the tape and do exercises 3 and 4 in your book.

5. Look at these sentences.
   - Did David go to football practice already?
   - No, he is going to go now.

   Listen to the question with **already**. Then write the answer with **now**.

   a. Did David play football already?
   b. Did he take pictures already?
   c. Did he have chicken already?
   d. Did he pick it up already?
   e. Did he eat already?
   f. Did his mother call already?
   g. Did she order it already?
   h. Did he pay for it already?

6. Look at this question and answer.
   - Is he going to football practice now?
   - No, he won't go until 4:30.

   Listen to the questions and write the answers. Use **until 4:30**.

   a. Is he going to school now?
   b. Is he playing football now?
   c. Is he taking pictures now?
   d. Is he having dinner now?
   e. Is he eating now?
   f. Is his mother calling now?
   g. Is David paying for dinner now?
   h. Is he picking it up now?
   i. Are they having fried chicken now?

Lesson 18: I'm Going to Quit *page 88*

Marla and Tom play tennis together. They always win. Now Tom is mad. Do you know why?

Tom: Marla! You are late again.

Marla: So?

Tom: If we don't practice, we'll lose.

Marla: We never lose.

Tom: We'll lose. Next Thursday we are playing Jason and Kevin.

Marla: So?

Tom: We'll lose. They are good.

Marla: They were good. They beat us last year. We will beat them this year.

Tom: If you get to practice on time, we will have a chance.

Marla: If you stop yelling and start playing, we will have a better chance.

Tom: I'm going to quit.

Marla: Quit. There are a hundred good tennis players in this town.

Tom: And every one of them is going to want to play tennis with you.

Marla: I only need one. Are you going to talk some more, or are we going to play tennis?

1. Listen to the questions. Circle **yes** or **no**.
   a. Is Marla late?
   b. Does Marla play with Tom?
   c. Is Jason good?
   d. Is Tom happy?
   e. Does Tom want to quit?
   f. If Tom quits, will Marla quit?
   g. Will someone else play tennis with Marla?
   h. Does Marla want to play tennis now?

2. Listen to the questions. For each question, circle the number of the correct answer.
   a. Who plays tennis with Marla?
   b. Who plays tennis with Jason?
   c. When are Marla and Tom playing Jason and Kevin?
   d. Who won last year?
   e. Who is late?
   f. Who is yelling?
   g. Who wants to play?
   h. Who thinks they will win?
   i. Who plays tennis in this town?
   j. Who says he is going to quit?

3. Listen to the questions. Circle **Tom** or **Marla**.
   a. Who is late again?
   b. Who thinks they are going to lose?
   c. Who thinks they are going to win?
   d. Who says Jason and Kevin are good?
   e. Who says Jason and Kevin were good?
   f. Who wants to start playing?
   g. Who talks about quitting?
   h. Who says there are other tennis players?

4. Listen to the beginning of each sentence. Circle the correct ending.
   a. If Marla is late again, Tom will be
   b. If they don't practice, they will
   c. If they are good, they will
   d. If they get to practice on time, they will
   e. If he stops yelling, they can
   f. If they start playing, they will
   g. If he quits, she will
   h. If she looks for another tennis player, she will

5. Look at these sentences.
   - Marla got to practice late again.
   - No, she didn't. But she will.

   Listen to the first sentence. Write a response.
   a. Marla practiced a lot.
   b. Tom got mad.
   c. Tom and Marla won.
   d. Kevin and Jason played well.
   e. Tom yelled a lot.
   f. He quit.
   g. Marla looked for another tennis player.
   h. Other players wanted to play.
   i. Tom talked some more.
   j. Tom and Marla played tennis.

6. Look at this question and answer.
   - Did they play well?
   - No, and they aren't going to, either.

   Listen to the questions and write the answers.
   a. Did she come to practice on time?
   b. Did they lose?
   c. Did he get mad?
   d. Did they play Jason and Kevin?
   e. Did they beat them?
   f. Did they start playing?
   g. Did he stop yelling?
   h. Did he quit?
   i. Did she find another tennis player?

Lesson 19: Are You Going to Go Back to Your Country? *page 92*

Peter Paul is in school in the United States. He looks very unhappy one day. Why is he so unhappy?

(classroom noise)

Teacher: Children, clean off your desks and line up for art.

(more shuffling)

Teacher: When you are quiet, you will be able to go.

(noise fades)

Teacher: Go ahead. Peter Paul, may I see you for a minute? *(pause)* Peter Paul, you don't look happy. Is something wrong?

Peter Paul: No.

Teacher: You are not going to tell me? *(pause)* Are you going to go back to your country?

Peter Paul: Yes.

Teacher: And you are going to miss us?

Peter Paul: Yes.

Teacher: But you are going to be with your family. That is good, isn't it?

Peter Paul: Yes.

Teacher: Are you coming back, or will you stay there?

Peter Paul: I will be back, but not here. My mother has a job in Texas. She will be going there in six months, and we will be going in one year.

Teacher: Will you send us a postcard?

Peter Paul: Yes. May I go to art now?

Teacher: Sure!

1. Listen to the questions. Circle **yes** or **no**.
    a. Is Peter Paul in school?
    b. Is the class going to gym?
    c. Does Peter Paul look happy?
    d. Is Peter Paul staying in the United States?
    e. Is he going back to his country?
    f. Is he going to miss his class?
    g. Is he going to be with his family?
    h. Is he staying there?
    i. Is his mother coming back to the United States?
    j. Is he going to send a postcard?

2. Listen to the questions. For each question, circle the number of the correct answer.
   a. Where is Peter Paul?
   b. Where is he going when he leaves the United States?
   c. Where will he go after that?
   d. Where is his class?
   e. Where is his mother going to work?
   f. Where is Peter Paul going in one year?
   g. To whom will he send a postcard?
   h. Where is he going right now?

3. Listen to these questions. Complete the answers.
   a. Where are Peter Paul and his teacher talking?
   b. Where are the children in the class going right now?
   c. Where will Peter Paul go?
   d. Where will he be with his family?
   e. Where will his mother work?
   f. Where will Peter Paul and his family go when they come back to the United States?
   g. Where is Peter Paul going after he talks to his teacher?

Now stop the tape and do exercise 4 in your book. If you need help with exercise 4, go back and listen to the conversation again.

5. Look at these sentences.
   - Did Peter Paul go back already?
   - No, he is going to go back next week.

   Listen to the question with **already**. Then write the answer with **next week**.
   a. Did he clean off his desk already?
   b. Did they line up for art already?
   c. Did the teacher talk to Peter Paul already?
   d. Did he go back to his country already?
   e. Did he go to art already?
   f. Did he send them a postcard already?

6. Look at these sentences.
   - Was he unhappy?
   - No, but he will be.

   Listen to the questions and write the answers.
   a. Was he in class?
   b. Were they in line?
   c. Were they quiet?
   d. Was there something wrong?
   e. Is he back?
   f. Is she working?
   g. Are they together?
   h. Was he writing?
   i. Is he in art?

Lesson 20: Why Won't You Lend Me Three Thousand Dollars? *page 95*

Allan won't lend Bob three thousand dollars. What can't Bob do now?

(a telephone rings)

Bob: Hello.
Allan: Hi. This is Allan. Is Bob there?
Bob: Hi, Al, this is Bob.
Allan: I have your answer. You are going to be mad.
Bob: Why am I going to be mad? You are going to lend me the money, aren't you?
Allan: No.
Bob: Why not?
Allan: Three thousand dollars is a lot of money.
Bob: I'll give it back to you in five weeks. What are brothers for?
Allan: I want to go to Nassau this month.
Bob: I owe Dad three thousand dollars. He needs the money.
Allan: Pay him in five weeks.
Bob: He needs the money now.
Allan: I'm sorry, Bob. I really need a vacation.

1. Listen to the questions. Circle **yes** or **no**.
    a. Allan and Bob are cousins.
    b. Bob wants money.
    c. Allan wants to borrow money.
    d. Bob needs five dollars.
    e. Allan will give Bob the money in five weeks.
    f. Bob can give the money back in five weeks.
    g. Bob wants to go to Nassau.
    h. Allan wants to go to Nassau.
    i. Bob owes Allan money.
    j. Bob owes his father money.
    k. Bob's father needs the money in five weeks.

2. Listen to the questions. For each question, circle the number of the correct answer.
    a. What does Allan want to do?
    b. What does Bob want to do?
    c. Where does Allan want to go?
    d. How much money does Bob owe?
    e. Who owes whom?
    f. Who wants to borrow money?
    g. Who borrowed money?
    h. Who lent money?
    i. Who doesn't want to lend money?

Now stop the tape and do exercise 3 in your book. If you need help with exercise 3, go back and listen to the conversation again.

4. Listen to the sentences. Circle **yes**, **no**, or **maybe**.
    a. Allan is going to be mad.
    b. Bob is going to lend Allan money.
    c. Bob is going to Nassau.
    d. Allan's father needs money.
    e. Bob wants to give the money back to Allan in five weeks.
    f. Allan will give his father the money in five weeks.
    g. Allan will give his father the money now.
    h. Allan wants to go to Nassau.
    i. Bob needs a vacation.
    j. Allan is going to lend Bob money.
    k. Bob is going to pay his father back.

5. Look at these sentences.
    - Did Bob borrow money five weeks ago?
    - No, but he is going to borrow money in five weeks.

    Listen to the question with **five weeks ago**. Then write the answer with **in five weeks**.
    a. Did Bob go to Nassau five weeks ago?
    b. Did Allan lend Bob money five weeks ago?
    c. Did Allan's father borrow money five weeks ago?
    d. Did Bob borrow money five weeks ago?
    e. Did Allan call Bob five weeks ago?
    f. Did he borrow $3,000 five weeks ago?
    g. Did he pay it back five weeks ago?

6. Look at these sentences.
    - Bob borrowed money.
    - No, he didn't. But he is going to.

    Listen to each sentence. Write the response.
    a. Allan borrowed money.
    b. Allan and Bob went to Nassau.
    c. Bob went to Nassau.
    d. Bob and Allan's sister lent them money.
    e. She went to Nassau.
    f. He owed his father money.
    g. They paid it back.
    h. She paid them.
    i. He paid her.
    j. We gave it back.

Unit 4

Lesson 21: We Got a New Teacher Yesterday *page 101*

Tina and Anabel are talking on the phone. They are in fifth grade in different schools. Tina got a new teacher yesterday. Why doesn't she like him?

(fade in, on phone)

Tina: ...so we can talk more about it at the movies on Saturday, okay?

Anabel: Sure. Anything else new?

Tina: Yes, I forgot to tell you. We got a new teacher yesterday.

Anabel: What happened to Ms. Chin?

Tina: She left. She got a job as director of training in the largest computer company in the world.

Anabel: I'm not surprised. She knows a lot about education. So what is the new teacher like?

Tina: First of all, he is ugly.

Anabel: Oh, Tina, tell me something important.

Tina: Well, he is probably a good teacher, but nobody likes him. We all miss Ms. Chin... *(fade out)*

Now stop the tape and do exercise 1 in your book.

2. Listen to the definitions. Write the words.
   a. did not remember
   b. person in charge, leader
   c. want to see
   d. maybe
   e. teaching, preparing for a job
   f. good to know
   g. a group of people who work together
   h. bad to look at
   i. the field of learning and teaching.

3. Listen to the questions. Write the answers.
   a. Who is talking on the phone?
   b. Who has a new teacher?
   c. Who is going to the movies?
   d. Who is Ms. Chin?
   e. Who knows a lot about education?
   f. Who is probably a good teacher?

4. Listen to the conversation again. Write the missing words.

   Tina: ...so we can talk more about it at the movies on Saturday, okay? *(pause)*
   Anabel: Sure. Anything else new?
   Tina: Yes, I forgot to tell you. *(pause)* We got a new teacher yesterday. *(pause)*
   Anabel: What happened to Ms. Chin? *(pause)*
   Tina: She left. She got a job as director of training in the largest computer company in the world. *(pause)*
   Anabel: I'm not surprised. She knows a lot about education. *(pause)* So what is the new teacher like? *(pause)*
   Tina: First of all, he is ugly.
   Anabel: Oh, Tina, tell me something important. *(pause)*
   Tina: Well, he is probably a good teacher, but nobody likes him. *(pause)* We all miss Ms. Chin...

5. Listen to the questions. For each question, circle the number of the correct answer.
    a. What are Tina and Anabel doing on Saturday?
    b. Why did Ms. Chin leave?
    c. Where will she work?
    d. What does she know a lot about?
    e. What do we know about the new teacher?
    f. Does Anabel want to know what he looks like?
    g. Who likes the new teacher?
    h. How do the children feel about Ms. Chin?

6. Listen to the statements. Write **T** if the statement is true. Write **F** if the statement is false.
    a. Tina and her teacher are talking.
    b. Tina and Anabel are talking.
    c. Tina has a new teacher.
    d. Anabel has a new teacher.
    e. Ms. Chin left.
    f. Ms. Chin was a good teacher.
    g. They are going to the movies with Ms. Chin.
    h. They are going to the movies on Saturday.

7. Underline the sentence you hear.
    a. We can talk more about it.
    b. I forgot to tell you.
    c. She got a new job.
    d. She knows a lot about training.
    e. He is probably a good teacher.
    f. We all miss Ms. Chin.

8. Read these sentences. Listen to the tape. Find the sentence that means the same as the one you hear. Write the correct letter on the line.
   a. Anything else new?
   b. I forgot to tell you.
   c. What happened to Ms. Chin?
   d. She left.
   e. I'm not surprised.
   f. She knows a lot about education.
   g. What is the new teacher like?
   h. He is ugly.
   i. We miss Ms. Chin.

Now stop the tape and do exercises 9 and 10 in your book.

Lesson 22: I Came to Register My Brother *page 107*

Guillermo Ortega, his father, and his brother Rafael are at school to register Guillermo. Who speaks English, and who does not?

Woman: Hello.

Rafael: Hello. I came to register my brother.

Woman: Good. Who else is with you?

Rafael: This is my father.

Woman: Hi! Let me talk to *you*.

Rafael: He doesn't speak English.

Woman: Oh. What is your brother's name?

Rafael: Guillermo Ortega.

Woman: How old is he?

Rafael: Twelve.

Woman: Where did he go to school before?

Rafael: In Spain.

Woman: Do you have his records?

Rafael: They gave us some of them. They are sending you the official ones.

Woman: Did he study English in Spain?

Rafael: He had English one hour a week in school, and he took private lessons two times a week.

Woman: When did he come here?

Rafael: Three days ago.

Woman: Fill out these forms and give them back to me. Tell your father we are happy he came to school with Guillermo. He can go to English classes if he wants to. They meet across the street in the library on Monday, Tuesday, Wednesday, and Thursday, from nine to eleven every morning.

Rafael: What do they cost?

Woman: They are free.

Now stop the tape and do exercise 1 in your book.

2. Listen to the definitions. Write the words.
    a. complete forms in order to go to a school
    b. grown-ups
    c. lists of a student's classes and grades
    d. containing the seal of the student and a director's signature
    e. not babies, not children

3. Listen to the questions. Write the answers.
    a. Who speaks English?
    b. Who doesn't speak English?
    c. Who came to register for school?
    d. Who is Guillermo's brother?
    e. Who went to school in Spain?
    f. Who studied English in Spain?
    g. Who came here three days ago?

4. Listen to the conversation again. Write the missing words.

Woman: Hello.

Rafael: Hello. I came to register my brother. *(pause)*

Woman: Good. Who else is with you? *(pause)*

Rafael: This is my father.

Woman: Hi! Let me talk to *you*. *(pause)*

Rafael: He doesn't speak English.

Woman: Oh. What is your brother's name?

Rafael: Guillermo Ortega.

Woman: How old is he? *(pause)*

Rafael: Twelve.

Woman: Where did he go to school before? *(pause)*

Rafael: In Spain.

Woman: Do you have his records?

Rafael: They gave us some of them. *(pause)* They are sending you the official ones.

Woman: Did he study English in Spain?

Rafael: He had English one hour a week in school, and he took private lessons two times a week. *(pause)*

Woman: When did he come here?

Rafael: Three days ago.

Woman: Fill out these forms and give them back to me. *(pause)* Tell your father we are happy he came to school with Guillermo. He can go to English classes if he wants to. *(pause)* They meet across the street in the library on Monday, Tuesday, Wednesday, and Thursday, from nine to eleven every morning.

Rafael: What do they cost? *(pause)*

Woman: They are free.

5. Listen to the questions. For each question, circle the number of the correct answer.
   a. How many people came to school with Guillermo?
   b. How old is Guillermo?
   c. How many times a week did Guillermo study English in Spain?
   d. When did Guillermo come here?
   e. Who is at school with Guillermo?
   f. Where are the English classes for adults?
   g. When are these adult classes?
   h. How much do the adult English classes cost?
   i. What time are the adult English classes?

6. Listen to the statements. Write **T** if the statement is true. Write **F** if the statement is false.
   a. Guillermo's father speaks English.
   b. Guillermo is twelve years old.
   c. Guillermo comes from Mexico.
   d. They have the official records with them.
   e. He came here three days ago.
   f. They have to fill out forms.
   g. The school has information on adult classes.
   h. Adult English classes cost a lot.

7. Underline the sentence you hear.
   a. This is my father.
   b. He doesn't speak English.
   c. They are sending you the official ones.
   d. Fill out these forms.
   e. Tell your father we are happy he is here.
   f. He can go to classes if he wants to.
   g. They meet in the library on Monday, Tuesday, Wednesday, and Thursday.
   h. They are free.

8. Read these sentences. Listen to the tape. Find the sentence that means the same as the one you hear. Write the correct letter on the line.
   a. He can go to English classes.
   b. Let me talk to *you*.
   c. How old is he?
   d. They gave us some of his papers.
   e. Do you have his records?
   f. When did he come here?
   g. He took private lessons two times a week.
   h. Where did he go to school before?
   i. What do they cost?
   j. I am here to register my brother.

Now stop the tape and do exercises 9 and 10 in your book.

Lesson 23: Are You Going to Buy a Wheelchair or Rent One? *page 114*

Luke and Corinne are cousins. They are at Luke's house, and Luke is telling Corinne about Brady, another cousin. What happened to Brady?

Corinne: So then what happened?

Luke: He went for a jump shot, made it, and landed wrong. He didn't get up. He broke his right leg in two places and injured his left ankle.

Corinne: What a mess! Can he walk?

Luke: Walk? He couldn't get out of bed for two days. He is coming to live with us until he is better.

Corinne: Are you going to buy a wheelchair or rent one?

Luke: Rent. They are very expensive, and his doctor says he will be walking in a month.

Corinne: Why is he coming to stay here? Can't he stay home in Manchester?

Luke: Sure. But Manchester was playing us when it happened, so he was taken to County Hospital here in Black Ridge. It will be easier to bring him here when he leaves the hospital than to drive him all the way to Manchester.

Now stop the tape and do exercise 1 in your book.

2. Listen to the definitions. Write the words.
   a. not cheap
   b. pay to keep something awhile
   c. problem
   d. chair on wheels
   e. a basketball shot
   f. hurt
   g. came down from a jump

3. Listen to the questions. Write the answers.
   a. When did he fall?
   b. When did he break his leg?
   c. When was he in bed?
   d. When is he coming to Luke's house?
   e. When will he be walking?
   f. When is he going back home?
   g. When did he go to County Hospital?

4. Listen to the conversation again. Write the missing words.

Corinne: So then what happened? *(pause)*

Luke: He went for a jump shot, made it, and landed wrong. *(pause)* He didn't get up. He broke his right leg in two places and injured his left ankle. *(pause)*

Corinne: What a mess! Can he walk? *(pause)*

Luke: Walk? He couldn't get out of bed for two days. He is coming to live with us until he is better. *(pause)*

Corinne: Are you going to buy a wheelchair or rent one? *(pause)*

Luke: Rent. They are very expensive, and his doctor says he will be walking in a month. *(pause)*

Corinne: Why is he coming to stay here? *(pause)* Can't he stay home in Manchester?

Luke: Sure. But Manchester was playing us when it happened, so he was taken to County Hospital here in Black Ridge. *(pause)* It will be easier to bring him here when he leaves the hospital than to drive him all the way to Manchester.

5. Listen to the questions. For each question, circle the number of the correct answer.
   a. When did Brady get hurt?
   b. When did he land wrong?
   c. How long was he in bed?
   d. When is he coming to live with Luke?
   e. When will he be walking?
   f. Where is Brady's home?
   g. Where does Luke live?
   h. Where are Luke and Corinne talking?

6. Listen to the statements. Write **T** if the statement is true. Write **F** if the statement is false.
   a. Luke and Corinne are brother and sister.
   b. Luke is at Corinne's house.
   c. Brady is their cousin.
   d. Brady plays baseball.
   e. Brady broke his leg.
   f. Brady hurt his ankle.
   g. Brady can't walk.
   h. Brady is going to stay at Luke's house.
   i. Luke lives in Oak Ridge.
   j. Wheelchairs are expensive.

7. Underline the sentence you hear.
   a. He can't walk.
   b. He went for a jump shot.
   c. He broke his leg in two places.
   d. Can he walk?
   e. He will be walking in a month.
   f. Why is he staying here?
   g. Can't he stay home?

8. Read these sentences. Listen to the tape. Find the sentence that means the same as the one you hear. Write the correct letter on the line.
   a. Why is he staying here?
   b. So then what happened?
   c. Manchester was playing us when it happened.
   d. He didn't get up.
   e. Can he walk?
   f. Sure.
   g. They are very expensive.

Now stop the tape and do exercises 9 and 10 in your book.

Lesson 24: If You Don't Open Your Mouth and Answer Me, I'm Leaving! *page 120*

Don and Howard are brothers. Don wants Howard to do something. Is Howard going to help him?

(door slams, footsteps)

Don: Howard, I'm glad you are home.

Howard: Hi, Don. How was your class?

Don: Okay. You are just the person I want to see.

Howard: How come?

Don: I have to type a seventy-five-page report for tomorrow.

Howard: Are you kidding?

Don: No, and you can help me.

Howard: Mmm.

Don: Will you?

Howard: I don't know.

Don: Well, what is there to think about? I helped you with your report in February. Remember?

Howard: No seventy-five pages.

Don: You do twenty-five, I do fifty.

Howard: No way.

Don: You use the word processor. I'll use the typewriter. *(pause)* Come on. *(pause)* Will you? *(pause)* If you don't open your mouth and answer me, I'm leaving.

Howard: Oh, yes?

Now stop the tape and do exercise 1 in your book.

2. Listen to the definitions. Write the words.
   a. machine for writing
   b. written discussion of a topic
   c. happy
   d. joking
   e. exactly
   f. write on a machine

3. Listen to the questions. Write the answers.
   a. Who is Don's brother?
   b. Who has a report to type?
   c. Who wants Howard's help?
   d. Who is not kidding?
   e. Who helped Howard in February?
   f. Who has a word processor?
   g. Who says he will leave?

4. Listen to the conversation again. Write the missing words.

Don: Howard, I'm glad you are home. *(pause)*
Howard: Hi, Don. How was your class?
Don: Okay. You are just the person I want to see. *(pause)*
Howard: How come?
Don: I have to type a seventy-five-page report for tomorrow. *(pause)*
Howard: Are you kidding?
Don: No, and you can help me. *(pause)*
Howard: Mmm.
Don: Will you?
Howard: I don't know.
Don: Well, what is there to think about? I helped you with your report in February. *(pause)* Remember?
Howard: No seventy-five pages.
Don: You do twenty-five, I do fifty. *(pause)*
Howard: No way.
Don: You use the word processor. *(pause)* I'll use the typewriter. *(pause)* Come on. Will you? If you don't open your mouth and answer me, I'm leaving. *(pause)*
Howard: Oh, yes?

5. Listen to the questions. For each question, circle the number of the correct answer.
    a. Who just came home?
    b. Who wants to see Howard?
    c. Who has to do a report?
    d. Who helped whom in February?
    e. Who had a report to do in February?
    f. Who wants Howard's help?

6. Listen to the statements. Write **T** if the statement is true. Write **F** if the statement is false.
    a. Don and Howard live together.
    b. They have a typewriter and a word processor.
    c. Howard's report is due tomorrow.
    d. Don wants Howard to type fifty pages.
    e. Howard wants to help Don.
    f. Don will use the word processor.
    g. Don helped Howard in February.
    h. Don gets mad.

7. Underline the sentence you hear.
    a. I'm glad you are home.
    b. You are just the person I want to see.
    c. How come?
    d. Are you kidding?
    e. You can help me.
    f. What is there to think about?
    g. You do twenty-five, I do fifty.
    h. You use the word processor.

8. Read these sentences. Listen to the tape. Find the sentence that means the same as the one you hear. Write the correct letter on the line.
    a. I'm happy you are here.
    b. I want your help.
    c. Why?
    d. That was no seventy-five pages.
    e. Not a chance.
    f. I'm going.
    g. Are you joking?
    h. Do you remember?
    i. I am not sure.

Now stop the tape and do exercises 9 and 10 in your book.

Lesson 25: A Pain in My Shoulder, an Earache, and My Arm Hurts *page 126*

Pete Caravella wants to see Dr. Rubin. Why does he want to see her? Does he need help right away?

Woman: Dr. Rubin's office, Megan speaking.
Pete: I want to see Dr. Rubin.
Woman: Are you a patient of ours?
Pete: No, I am not.
Woman: What is the problem?
Pete: I have a pain in my shoulder, an earache, and my arm hurts.
Woman: Which side?
Pete: The right.
Woman: Do you want to make an appointment?
Pete: Yes.
Woman: Thursday morning at 9:45.
Pete: I can't come in then.
Woman: Then next Monday at 10:00.
Pete: I work.
Woman: How about Tuesday at 4:00?
Pete: I work until 6:00.
Woman: Tuesday at 8:00?
Pete: Good. What does the first visit cost?
Woman: Forty-five dollars. May I have your name, please?
Pete: Pete Caravella.
Woman: Your telephone number?
Pete: 555-7622.
Woman: Home or work?
Pete: Home.
Woman: What is your telephone number at work?
Pete: 555-4800, extension 302.
Woman: We will see you Tuesday, April 10, at 8:00 in the evening.
Pete: How do I get there?
Woman: Where are you coming from?
Pete: Fairfield.
Woman: West on 38 to Downing Road. Right on Downing Road. The second stoplight is Plaque Boulevard. Turn left on Plaque. We are the third building on the right, number 2811. Parking is in the rear.
Pete: West on 38, right on Downing, left on Plaque to 2811.
Woman: That's right.
Pete: Thank you.
Woman: Good-bye.
Pete: Bye.

Now stop the tape and do exercise 1 in your book.

2. Listen to the definitions. Write the words.
   a. a pain in the ear
   b. in back, behind a building
   c. not the top, not the bottom, not the front, not the back
   d. a box with lights that mean *stop*, *wait*, and *go*
   e. the time a patient spends with a doctor
   f. a person who goes to a doctor
   g. the body part at the top of the arm
   h. a time to see someone

3. Listen to the questions. Write the answers.
   a. What is the doctor's name?
   b. What is the patient's problem?
   c. What is the patient's name?
   d. What is the patient's telephone number at home?
   e. What is the doctor's address?

4. Listen to the conversation again. Write the missing words.

Woman: Dr. Rubin's office, Megan speaking.
Pete: I want to see Dr. Rubin. *(pause)*
Woman: Are you a patient of ours? *(pause)*
Pete: No, I am not.
Woman: What is the problem?
Pete: I have a pain in my shoulder, an earache, and my arm hurts. *(pause)*
Woman: Which side?
Pete: The right.
Woman: Do you want to make an appointment?
Pete: Yes.
Woman: Thursday morning at 9:45. *(pause)*
Pete: I can't come in then.
Woman: Then next Monday at 10:00. *(pause)*
Pete: I work.
Woman: How about Tuesday at 4:00? *(pause)*
Pete: I work until 6:00.
Woman: Tuesday at 8:00?
Pete: Good. What does the first visit cost? *(pause)*
Woman: Forty-five dollars. May I have your name, please?
Pete: Pete Caravella.
Woman: Your telephone number?
Pete: 555–7622. *(pause)*
Woman: Home or work?
Pete: Home.
Woman: What is your telephone number at work?
Pete: 555–4800, extension 302. *(pause)*

Woman: We will see you Tuesday, April 10, at 8:00 in the evening.
Pete: How do I get there?
Woman: Where are you coming from?
Pete: Fairfield.
Woman: West on 38 to Downing Road. Right on Downing Road. *(pause)* The second stoplight is Plaque Boulevard. Turn left on Plaque. *(pause)* We are the third building on the right, number 2811. *(pause)* Parking is in the rear.
Pete: West on 38, right on Downing, left on Plaque to 2811.
Woman: That's right.
Pete: Thank you.
Woman: Good-bye.
Pete: Bye.

5. Listen to the questions. For each question, circle the number of the correct answer.
   a. What is the doctor's name?
   b. What is the patient's problem?
   c. What is the patient's name?
   d. What is the patient's telephone number at home?
   e. What is the patient's telephone number at work?
   f. What is the doctor's address?

6. Listen to the statements. Write **T** if the statement is true. Write **F** if the statement is false.
   a. The patient wants to see Dr. Rubin.
   b. The patient wants to see Dr. Megan.
   c. The patient has pain on the left side.
   d. The patient works until 6:00.
   e. The appointment is Tuesday at 8:00.
   f. The first visit costs $40.00.
   g. Dr. Rubin's office is on Downing Road.

7. Underline the sentence or phrase you hear.
   a. I want to see Dr. Rubin.
   b. Thursday morning at 9:45
   c. next Monday at 6:00
   d. What is the problem?
   e. What is your telephone number?
   f. Where is your office?

8. Read these sentences. Listen to the tape. Find the sentence that means the same as the one you hear. Write the correct letter on the line.
   a. I have a pain in my shoulder.
   b. May I have your name, please?
   c. How about Tuesday at 4:00?
   d. That's right.
   e. Megan speaking.
   f. I want to see Dr. Rubin.
   g. What does the first visit cost?

Now stop the tape and do exercises 9 and 10 in your book.

Lesson 26: I Won't Say Hello Because She Never Says Hello *page 133*

Michelle and Kenneth work for Lynn in an auto parts store. Why doesn't Kenneth say hello to Lynn?

Michelle: Hi, Kenneth. I just saw Lynn.

Kenneth: So?

Michelle: She said she likes our work, but she is not crazy about your attitude.

Kenneth: Attitude? What attitude? I do my work. This place always looks good. The shelves are always full. The storeroom is clean. She can find anything she needs. It is a good place to shop.

Michelle: I know, Kenneth. I said she likes our work. How about being a nice person?

Kenneth: I smile at everyone. I say hello to everyone.

Michelle: Except Lynn.

Kenneth: She doesn't shop here. Why do I have to say hello to her?

Michelle: She gave you the job. She is the boss.

Kenneth: Bosses don't have to say hello?

Michelle: You say hello first.

Kenneth: I won't say hello because she never says hello.

Now stop the tape and do exercise 1 in your book.

2. Listen to the definitions. Write the words.
   a. flat places on which to put things
   b. parts for cars
   c. supervisor
   d. way of thinking and acting
   e. room in which to keep things
   f. like very much

3. Listen to the questions. Write the answers.
   a. Where does Michelle work?
   b. Where does Kenneth work?
   c. Who works for Lynn?
   d. Who is Lynn?
   e. How does the store look?
   f. What does Lynn like?
   g. What doesn't Lynn like?
   h. What is Kenneth's job?

4. Listen to the conversation again. Write the missing words.

Michelle: Hi, Kenneth. I just saw Lynn. *(pause)*

Kenneth: So?

Michelle: She said she likes our work, but she is not crazy about your attitude. *(pause)*

Kenneth: Attitude? What attitude? I do my work. *(pause)* This place always looks good. The shelves are always full. The storeroom is clean. She can find anything she needs. *(pause)* It is a good place to shop.

Michelle: I know, Kenneth. I said she likes our work. How about being a nice person?

Kenneth: I smile at everyone. *(pause)* I say hello to everyone.

Michelle: Except Lynn.

Kenneth: She doesn't shop here. *(pause)* Why do I have to say hello to her?

Michelle: She gave you the job. *(pause)* She is the boss.

Kenneth: Bosses don't have to say hello?

Michelle: You say hello first. *(pause)*

Kenneth: I won't say hello because she never says hello. *(pause)*

5. Listen to the questions. For each question, circle the number of the correct answer.
   a. Where do Michelle and Kenneth work?
   b. Who owns the store?
   c. Who is the boss?
   d. Does Lynn like Kenneth's work?
   e. Does Lynn like Kenneth's attitude?
   f. How does Kenneth do his job?
   g. When does Kenneth smile?
   h. Who gave Kenneth the job?
   i. Why doesn't Kenneth say hello to Lynn?

6. Listen to the statements. Write **T** if the statement is true. Write **F** if the statement is false.
   a. Lynn works for Kenneth.
   b. Michelle is the boss.
   c. Lynn likes Kenneth's work.
   d. The store sells auto parts.
   e. Lynn is crazy about Kenneth's attitude.
   f. Kenneth is not crazy about Lynn.
   g. Kenneth keeps the shelves full.
   h. He keeps the storeroom clean.
   i. Lynn's store is a bad place to shop.
   j. Kenneth has a bad attitude with shoppers.

7. Underline the sentence you hear.
   a. I just saw Lynn.
   b. She is not crazy about your attitude.
   c. Attitude? What attitude?
   d. The shelves are always full.
   e. It is a good place to shop.
   f. I say hello to everyone.
   g. She doesn't shop here.
   h. She gave you the job.
   i. You say hello first.

8. Read these sentences. Listen to the tape. Find the sentence that means the same as the one you hear. Write the correct letter on the line.
   a. Why doesn't he greet her?
   b. She is pleased with us.
   c. I do what I'm supposed to.
   d. Try to be pleasant.
   e. I always smile.
   f. She is not a customer.
   g. She employed you.
   h. Shouldn't bosses say hello?

Now stop the tape and do exercises 9 and 10 in your book.

Lesson 27: Did You Read the Book I Gave You? *page 140*

Julie and John are having lunch. Why didn't Julie finish the book John gave her?

John: Did you read the book I gave you?

Julie: John, you gave it to me two days ago. I went skating that night, had school yesterday, played tennis after school, ate dinner out with my aunt and uncle, had an evening soccer game, and was in school this morning. When did you think I was going to read?

John: Shirley, Jeff, and Joe are waiting to read it, so hurry up.

Julie: Give it to them first. Is this the only copy in the world?

John: No, but it is probably the only copy in North Dakota.

Julie: Shirley is busy building a garage with her father. Jeff and Joe are painting their uncle's house. They can wait. If it is the best book in the world, I will finish it by Monday.

John: Do you want to go to the movies tomorrow?

Julie: No, thanks. I have to read a book.

Now stop the tape and do exercise 1 in your book.

2. Listen to the definitions. Write the words.
   a. wanting
   b. the part of the day after dinner
   c. one of something
   d. supper
   e. be quick
   f. house for a car

3. Listen to the questions. Write the answers.
   a. What are Julie and John doing?
   b. When did John give Julie the book?
   c. When did Julie go skating?
   d. When did she play tennis?
   e. When did she go out for dinner?
   f. When did she play soccer?
   g. Did she read the book?
   h. Does Shirley want to read it?
   i. Does Jeff want to read it?
   j. What will Julie do tomorrow?

4. Listen to the conversation again. Write the missing words.

John: Did you read the book I gave you? *(pause)*

Julie: John, you gave it to me two days ago. I went skating that night, had school yesterday, played tennis after school, ate dinner out with my aunt and uncle, had an evening soccer game, and was in school this morning. *(pause)* When did you think I was going to read? *(pause)*

John: Shirley, Jeff, and Joe are waiting to read it, so hurry up. *(pause)*

Julie: Give it to them first. Is this the only copy in the world?

John: No, but it is probably the only copy in North Dakota. *(pause)*

Julie: Shirley is busy building a garage with her father. Jeff and Joe are painting their uncle's house. *(pause)* They can wait. If it is the best book in the world, I will finish it by Monday. *(pause)*

John: Do you want to go to the movies tomorrow? *(pause)*

Julie: No, thanks. I have to read a book. *(pause)*

5. Listen to the questions. Circle the number of the correct answer.
    a. Why did John give Julie a book?
    b. Why didn't Julie read the book?
    c. Why do Shirley, Jeff, and Joe want to read the book?
    d. Why can they wait?
    e. When will Julie finish reading the book?
    f. Why does John ask Julie to the movies?
    g. Why does Julie say no?

6. Listen to the statements. Write **T** if the statement is true. Write **F** if the statement is false.
    a. It is lunchtime.
    b. John gave Julie a book.
    c. Julie read the book.
    d. Shirley wants to read the book.
    e. Julie plays tennis.
    f. Julie goes to school.
    g. John lives in North Dakota.
    h. Jeff is making a garage.
    i. Joe is building a house.
    j. Julie can't go to the movies.

7. Underline the sentence you hear.
    a. Did you read the book?
    b. I got it two days ago.
    c. I went skating that night.
    d. I had dinner out with my uncle.
    e. When did you think I was going to read?
    f. Give it to them first.
    g. Jeff and Joe are painting their uncle's house.
    h. I will finish it by Monday.
    i. I have to read a book.

8. Read these sentences and phrases. Listen to the tape. Find the sentence that means the same as the one you hear. Write the correct letter on the line.
    a. out to dinner with them
    b. after school, tennis
    c. Let them wait.
    d. They want to read it.
    e. I got it from you the day before yesterday.
    f. Let them have it first.
    g. Is there another copy?
    h. They are eating lunch.
    i. She has something to do.

Now stop the tape and do exercises 9 and 10 in your book.

Lesson 28: Did You Tell Them We Are Not Inviting Them? *page 146*

Sheridan and Alistair are planning a party. Why aren't they inviting their next-door neighbors?

Sheridan: What time do you want me to tell people to come?
Alistair: Let's make it from seven to eleven.
Sheridan: Friday or Saturday?
Alistair: How about Sunday? Monday is a holiday.
Sheridan: What do we make, and what do we buy?
Alistair: You make some sandwiches. I will make a salad, and we can buy drinks, fruit, and ice cream.
Sheridan: How about ice cream from Hansen's?
Alistair: We aren't inviting them.
Sheridan: Did you tell them we aren't inviting them?
Alistair: No.
Sheridan: They live next door. Let's tell them.
Alistair: Why? We don't have to invite them every time we have people to our house.
Sheridan: That's right. And we can still have Hansen's ice cream at the party.
Alistair: Okay. I will get it Sunday afternoon.

Now stop the tape and do exercise 1 in your book.

2. Listen to the definitions. Write the words.
   a. have it
   b. asking to come
   c. people who live near you
   d. one house away
   e. what do you think about
   f. mixture of vegetables

3. Listen to the questions. Write the answers.
   a. What time is the party?
   b. What day is the party?
   c. Who is having a party?
   d. Where is the party?
   e. What are they going to make?
   f. What are they going to buy?
   g. Why aren't they inviting the Hansens?

4. Listen to the conversation again. Write the missing words.

Sheridan: What time do you want me to tell people to come? *(pause)*
Alistair: Let's make it from seven to eleven.
Sheridan: Friday or Saturday?
Alistair: How about Sunday? *(pause)* Monday is a holiday.
Sheridan: What do we make, and what do we buy? *(pause)*
Alistair: You make some sandwiches. I will make a salad, and we can buy drinks, fruit, and ice cream.
Sheridan: How about ice cream from Hansen's? *(pause)*
Alistair: We aren't inviting them. *(pause)*
Sheridan: Did you tell them we aren't inviting them?
Alistair: No.
Sheridan: They live next door. *(pause)* Let's tell them.
Alistair: Why? We don't have to invite them every time we have people to our house.
Sheridan: That's right. And we can still have Hansen's ice cream at the party. *(pause)*
Alistair: Okay. I will get it Sunday afternoon. *(pause)*

5. Listen to the questions. For each question, circle the number of the correct answer.
   a. What time is the party?
   b. When is the party?
   c. Why is the party Sunday?
   d. What are they making?
   e. What are they buying?
   f. Where are they getting the ice cream?
   g. Are they inviting the Hansens?
   h. Where do the Hansens live?
   i. When is Alistair going to get the ice cream?

6. Listen to the statements. Write **T** if the statement is true. Write **F** if the statement is false.
   a. Sheridan and Alistair are neighbors.
   b. They are having a party.
   c. The party is Saturday.
   d. They are making a salad.
   e. They are buying sandwiches.
   f. They are inviting the Hansens.
   g. They told the Hansens about the party.
   h. The Hansens live next door.
   i. They will get the ice cream at Hansen's.

7. Underline the sentence you hear.
   a. What time do you want to tell people to come?
   b. Let's make it at 7:00.
   c. How about Sunday? Monday is a holiday.
   d. We can buy drinks, fruit, and ice cream.
   e. We aren't inviting them.
   f. I will get it Sunday afternoon.

8. Read these sentences. Listen to the tape. Find the sentence that means the same as the one you hear. Write the correct letter on the line.
   a. Let's make it at seven.
   b. Friday or Saturday?
   c. Monday is a holiday.
   d. I will make a salad.
   e. How about ice cream?
   f. We aren't inviting them.
   g. They live next door.
   h. I will get it.

Now stop the tape and do exercises 9 and 10 in your book.

Lesson 29: Did She Say Why She Is Moving? *page 153*

Two friends are talking about Julia. Why is she going to move?

Sue: So did you see Julia today?
Bob: No, she is home packing.
Sue: When is she moving?
Bob: The day after tomorrow.
Sue: She won't be here for the art show on Thursday.
Bob: No, and she will miss the Sunday concert.
Sue: Did she say why she is moving?
Bob: Her parents run a private school, and she is going to live at the school.
Sue: Does she want to?
Bob: I think so. It is only thirty miles from here.
Sue: Over the mountain. In winter that is like a thousand miles.
Bob: You are going to miss her, aren't you?
Sue: Of course. So is everybody.

Now stop the tape and do exercise 1 in your book.

2. Listen to the definitions. Write the words.
   a. putting things into boxes
   b. time and place to see art
   c. not a public school
   d. naturally
   e. going to live in another place
   f. music show
   g. want to see

3. Listen to the questions. Write the answers.
   a. Who is going to move?
   b. Where is Julia today?
   c. Where is Julia going to live?
   d. Will Julia be here on Thursday?
   e. When is Julia moving?
   f. Who will miss Julia?

4. Listen to the conversation again. Write the missing words.

Sue: So did you see Julia today? *(pause)*
Bob: No, she is home packing.
Sue: When is she moving? *(pause)*
Bob: The day after tomorrow.
Sue: She won't be here for the art show on Thursday. *(pause)*
Bob: No, and she will miss the Sunday concert.
Sue: Did she say why she is moving? *(pause)*
Bob: Her parents run a private school, and she is going to live at the school. *(pause)*
Sue: Does she want to?
Bob: I think so. It is only thirty miles from here.
Sue: Over the mountain. In winter that is like a thousand miles. *(pause)*
Bob: You are going to miss her, aren't you? *(pause)*
Sue: Of course. So is everybody.

5. Listen to the questions. For each question, circle the number of the correct answer.
   a. Where was Julia today?
   b. When is she moving?
   c. When is the art show?
   d. When is the concert?
   e. Why is she moving?
   f. Where is she going to live?
   g. Where is the school?
   h. Where do you think these people are talking?

6. Listen to the statements. Write **T** if the statement is true. Write **F** if the statement is false.
   a. Julia moved today.
   b. The art show is on Friday.
   c. The concert is on Sunday.
   d. Julia's family has a school.
   e. The school is thirty miles away.
   f. Julia lives at the school now.
   g. Julia is moving very far away.
   h. Everyone will miss Julia.

7. Underline the sentence you hear.
    a. She is home packing.
    b. At 2:00 tomorrow.
    c. He won't be here.
    d. She will miss the Sunday concert.
    e. Her parents run a private school.
    f. Does she want to?
    g. Are you going to miss her?
    h. So is everybody.

8. Read these sentences. Listen to the tape. Find the sentence that means the same as the one you hear. Write the correct letter on the line.
    a. Did you see Julia today?
    b. She is home packing.
    c. When is she moving?
    d. The day after tomorrow.
    e. She won't be here for the concert.
    f. Did she say why she is moving?
    g. I think so.
    h. So is everybody.

Now stop the tape and do exercises 9 and 10 in your book.

Lesson 30: The Winter County Free Public Library *page 159*

Erik Steiner wants to see the library. What does he need?

Woman: May I help you?
  Erik: Yes. I need a library card.
Woman: Where do you live?
  Erik: Here in Rossburg.
Woman: Okay. Let me have your name.
  Erik: Erik Steiner.
Woman: Is that "Eric" with a "c"?
  Erik: No, "k," E-R-I-K.
Woman: And please spell "Steiner."
  Erik: S-T-E-I-N-E-R.
Woman: May I have your address?
  Erik: 1400 Brook Drive.
Woman: Is there any apartment number?
  Erik: Three twenty "A."
Woman: Three twenty-eight?
  Erik: No, three, two, zero, "A."
Woman: All right, and may I have your telephone number?
  Erik: 555–3142.
Woman: Here is your temporary card. Your permanent card will be ready in a week to ten days. We will send it to you.

Erik: Thank you. What are the library hours?
Woman: Monday to Thursday, nine to nine; Friday, nine to six; Saturday, ten to four. We're closed Sundays.
Erik: What is upstairs?
Woman: Those are reading rooms. They are for studying and reading.
Erik: Do you have a photocopy machine?
Woman: Yes. It is over there behind the children's section. Copies cost ten cents. There is a dollar changer next to the photocopy machine.
Erik: Okay. Thanks!

Now stop the tape and do exercise 1 in your book.

2. Listen to the definitions. Write the words.
   a. a machine that gives you change for a dollar
   b. a card that gives you permission to take books from the library
   c. only for a while
   d. a machine that makes copies
   e. forever
   f. on the second floor

3. Listen to the questions. Write the answers.
   a. Where is Erik?
   b. Where does Erik live?
   c. Where is the photocopy machine?
   d. Where is the dollar changer?

4. Listen to the conversation again. Write the missing words.

Woman: May I help you?
Erik: Yes. I need a library card. *(pause)*
Woman: Where do you live?
Erik: Here in Rossburg.
Woman: Okay. Let me have your name. *(pause)*
Erik: Erik Steiner.
Woman: Is that "Eric" with a "c"?
Erik: No, "k," E-R-I-K.
Woman: And please spell "Steiner."
Erik: S-T-E-I-N-E-R.
Woman: May I have your address? *(pause)*
Erik: 1400 Brook Drive.
Woman: Is there any apartment number?
Erik: Three twenty "A."
Woman: Three twenty-eight?
Erik: No, three, two, zero, "A."
Woman: All right, and may I have your telephone number? *(pause)*
Erik: 555-3142.

Woman: Here is your temporary card. *(pause)* Your permanent card will be ready in a week to ten days. *(pause)* We will send it to you.

Erik: Thank you. What are the library hours?

Woman: Monday to Thursday, nine to nine; Friday, nine to six; Saturday, ten to four. We're closed Sundays.

Erik: What is upstairs? *(pause)*

Woman: Those are reading rooms. They are for studying and reading.

Erik: Do you have a photocopy machine? *(pause)*

Woman: Yes. It is over there behind the children's section. Copies cost ten cents. There is a dollar changer next to the photocopy machine.

Erik: Okay. Thanks!

5. Listen to the questions. For each question, circle the number of the correct answer.
   a. What does Erik want?
   b. Where does Erik live?
   c. How do you spell "Erik"?
   d. What is Erik's address?
   e. What is Erik's apartment number?
   f. What is Erik's telephone number?
   g. When will Erik get a permanent library card?
   h. How will Erik get his permanent card?
   i. What are the library hours on Friday?
   j. When is the library closed?
   k. What is upstairs?
   l. What do photocopies cost?
   m. Where is the dollar changer?

6. Listen to the statements. Write **T** if the statement is true. Write **F** if the statement is false.
   a. Erik Steiner needs a library card.
   b. The library is in Brook County.
   c. Erik lives in an apartment.
   d. The library is closed on Saturdays.
   e. Reading rooms are upstairs.
   f. The library has a children's section.

7. Underline the sentence you hear.
   a. I need a library card.
   b. Give me your name.
   c. Please tell me your name.
   d. Is there any apartment number there?
   e. What are the library hours?
   f. We're closed Thursdays.
   g. We have a dollar changer.

8. Read these sentences. Listen to the tape. Find the sentence that means the same as the one you hear. Write the correct letter on the line.
   a. What is upstairs?
   b. Is that "Eric" with a "c"?
   c. May I help you?
   d. What are the library hours?
   e. May I have your telephone number?
   f. Let me have your name.
   g. Here is a temporary library card.
   h. Copies cost ten cents.

Now stop the tape and do exercises 9 and 10 in your book.

Answer Key

Contents

Unit 1
Lesson 1: I Am Happy That I Have a Sister ... 75
Lesson 2: I Am Not Chinese ... 76
Lesson 3: He Paints Houses for a Living, and Hates It ... 78
Lesson 4: You Always Look Tired ... 79
Lesson 5: They Don't Even Have a Movie Theater ... 81
Lesson 6: Anything Else? ... 82
Lesson 7: Can You Draw a Stegosaurus? ... 84
Lesson 8: Does the Sun Ever Come Out in Bergen? ... 85
Lesson 9: I Am Not Cut Out for Parachuting ... 86
Lesson 10: Call Back Later ... 88

Unit 2
Lesson 11: I Ate Too Much Pizza ... 90
Lesson 12: I Got a Cordless Phone for $6.99! ... 91
Lesson 13: Where Did You Buy Your Down Jacket? ... 92
Lesson 14: How Did You Break Your Elbow? ... 94
Lesson 15: This Soup Is Awful! Did You Forget the Salt? ... 95

Unit 3
Lesson 16: I Won't Be Back until August ... 97
Lesson 17: You Don't Play Football! ... 98
Lesson 18: I'm Going to Quit ... 99
Lesson 19: Are You Going to Go Back to Your Country? ... 100
Lesson 20: Why Won't You Lend Me Three Thousand Dollars? ... 101

Unit 4
Lesson 21: We Got a New Teacher Yesterday ... 103
Lesson 22: I Came to Register My Brother ... 104
Lesson 23: Are You Going to Buy a Wheelchair or Rent One? ... 105
Lesson 24: If You Don't Open Your Mouth and Answer Me, I'm Leaving! ... 107
Lesson 25: A Pain in My Shoulder, an Earache, and My Arm Hurts ... 108
Lesson 26: I Won't Say Hello Because She Never Says Hello ... 109
Lesson 27: Did You Read the Book I Gave You? ... 111
Lesson 28: Did You Tell Them We Are Not Inviting Them? ... 112
Lesson 29: Did She Say Why She Is Moving? ... 113
Lesson 30: The Winter County Free Public Library ... 114

Unit 1

Lesson 1: I Am Happy That I Have a Sister *page 3*

1. a. 1. He is a boy.
      2. He is Karah's brother.
      3. He is three.
      4. He is hitting Karah.
      5. He can walk.
      6. He can talk.
   b. 1. She is a girl.
      2. She is Noah's sister.
      3. She is nine months old.
      4. She is a baby.
      5. She can crawl.
      6. She can stand.
      7. She cannot walk.
      8. She can eat muffins.
   c. 1. She is Noah's cousin.
      2. She is Karah's cousin.
      3. She can bake.
      4. She wants Karah to eat muffins.

2. a. 1. a boy
   b. 3. a baby
   c. 1. Noah
   d. 2. Karah
   e. 3. Roberta
   f. 1. She is a baby.
   g. 2. Noah likes muffins.
   h. 1. He is bigger than Karah.
   i. 2. She can stand.
   j. 3. Karah

3. a. is
   b. are
   c. Give
   d. Help
   e. can't
   f. stand
   g. walk
   h. run
   i. Come
   j. have
   k. wants
   l. Can

4. a. Why can't Karah walk?
   b. Why can't Karah talk?
   c. Why can't Karah bake banana muffins?
   d. Why can't Karah help Noah up?
   e. Why can't Karah help Roberta up?

5. a. yes   e. yes
   b. no   f. yes
   c. yes   g. no
   d. no   h. yes

6. a. 1   d. 2
      2   1
   b. 2   e. 1
      1   2
   c. 1
      2

7. a. Karah stands.
   b. Karah hits.
   c. Karah eats.
   d. Karah sits in the sun.
   e. Karah eats banana muffins.

8. a. Noah is a boy.
   b. Noah likes muffins.
   c. Karah eats muffins.
   d. Karah is a baby.
   e. Roberta is Noah's cousin.
   f. Roberta can bake muffins.

Lesson 2: I Am Not Chinese *page 8*

1. a. 1. She is in class.
      2. She is at Central School.
      3. She is studying.
      4. Her husband is Chinese.
      5. Her father is a Quechua Indian.
      6. Her mother is Mexican.
      7. She is not Chinese.
      8. She does not speak Chinese.
      9. She speaks Spanish.
      10. She looks Chinese.
   b. 1. He is at Central School.
      2. He is in the office.
      3. He speaks Chinese.
      4. He wants some information.
   c. 1. There are classes there.
      2. There are English classes there.
      3. Rose studies there.
      4. Mr. Chen studies there.
      5. Central School is open at night.
      6. The office is open at night.

2. a. 3. at Central School   f. 1. Spanish
   b. 1. English   g. 1. Rose Wong's father
   c. 2. in the office   h. 1. Rose Wong's father
   d. 3. Chinese   i. 3. Rose Wong's husband
   e. 3. some information

3. a. is   i. can, help
   b. studies   j. ask, wants
   c. come   k. don't speak
   d. am, take   l. speak
   e. is   m. is
   f. speaks   n. look
   g. wants   o. happens
   h. Can, help

4. a. Does Rose study English?
   b. Does Rose go to the office?
   c. Can Mr. Chen speak English?
   d. Can Mr. Chen speak Chinese?
   e. Does Mr. Chen want information?
   f. Can Rose help Mr. Chen?
   g. Can Rose speak Chinese?

5. a. yes   d. no
   b. yes   e. yes
   c. no   f. no

6. a. 2   d. 2
      1   1
   b. 1   e. 1
      2   2
   c. 2
      1

7. a. He doesn't speak Japanese.
   b. He doesn't speak Japanese.
   c. He doesn't speak Japanese.
   d. She doesn't speak Japanese.
   e. She doesn't speak Japanese.
   f. He doesn't speak Japanese.
   g. He doesn't speak Japanese.

8. a. Rose studies English.
   b. Rose goes to school at night.
   c. Rose's husband is Chinese.
   d. Rose's father is Quechua.
   e. Rose's mother speaks Spanish.
   f. Mr. Chen speaks Chinese.

Lesson 3: He Paints Houses for a Living, and Hates It *page 13*

1. a. 1. She looks unhappy.
      2. She doesn't look happy.
      3. She doesn't feel happy.
      4. She feels unhappy.
   b. 1. He doesn't feel happy.
      2. He feels unhappy.
      3. He has too much work.
      4. He doesn't have enough money.
      5. He doesn't teach school.
      6. He doesn't load trucks.
      7. He paints houses.
      8. He hates his job.
   c. 1. He lives near Lucy
      2. He sees Lucy outside.
      3. He stops to talk to her.

2. a. 2. on the same street
   b. 3. unhappy
   c. 3. unhappy
   d. 2. too much work
   e. 1. He paints houses.
   f. 3. He hates it.

3. a. is   f. has
   b. know   g. does, do
   c. don't look   h. teach
   d. feel   i. Does, load
   e. doesn't   j. looks

4. a. Why isn't Lucy happy?
   b. Why is Lucy unhappy?
   c. Why isn't Lucy's father happy?
   d. Why is Lucy's father unhappy?
   e. Why isn't Lucy's father a teacher?
   f. Why is Lucy's father a painter?

5. a. yes   f. no
   b. no   g. no
   c. no   h. yes
   d. yes   i. no
   e. no

6. a. 2   c. 2
      1   1
   b. 1
      2

7. a. Lucy sees Terry.
   b. Lucy talks.
   c. Lucy looks unhappy.
   d. Lucy feels unhappy.
   e. Lucy works too much.

8. a. Lucy and Terry live on the same street.
   b. Terry talks to Lucy.
   c. Lucy doesn't look happy.
   d. Lucy doesn't feel happy.
   e. Lucy's father doesn't feel happy.
   f. He works too hard.
   g. He paints houses.
   h. He hates his job.

Lesson 4: You Always Look Tired *page 18*

1. a. 1. She works in a restaurant.
      2. She cooks in a restaurant.
      3. She goes to school.
      4. She wants some soup.
      5. She works with Nancy.
      6. She works after school.
      7. She says Nancy looks tired.
   b. 1. She works in a restaurant.
      2. She goes to school.
      3. She feels like a salad.
      4. She has a lot of homework.
      5. She takes care of the house.
      6. She looks tired.
   c. 1. Joelle is the cook.
      2. Nancy is the cashier.
      3. They have soup.
      4. They have salad.
      5. They are not busy.

2. a. 1. Joelle and Nancy
   b. 1. Joelle
   c. 2. Nancy
   d. 2. Nancy
   e. 2. Nancy's parents
   f. 2. Nancy's parents
   g. 1. Nancy
   h. 2. Nancy

3. a. work h. are
   b. cooks i. takes
   c. is j. has
   d. are k. are
   e. wants l. is
   f. feels m. are
   g. has n. looks

4. a. Does she work?
   b. Does she want to eat?
   c. Does she have a lot of homework?
   d. Does she take care of the house?
   e. Does she have sisters?
   f. Does she look tired?

5. a. yes f. yes
   b. yes g. yes
   c. yes h. no
   d. no i. yes
   e. no

6. a. 1 e. 2
      2   1
   b. 2 f. 1
      1   2
   c. 2 g. 2
      1   1
   d. 1
      2

7. a. Do you feel like a salad?
   b. Do you cook?
   c. Do you look tired?
   d. Do you want some soup?
   e. Do you get a lot of homework?
   f. Do you take care of the house?

8. a. She works in a restaurant.
   b. She is a cashier.
   c. She wants a salad.
   d. She has a lot of homework.
   e. She takes care of the house.
   f. She has sisters.
   g. She looks tired
   h. Her parents are away.
   i. They are on a ship.
   j. They are on the Nile.
   k. They are always busy.

Lesson 5: They Don't Even Have a Movie Theater *page 23*

1. a. 1. She is moving.
       2. She likes Franklin.
       3. She plays soccer.
       4. She likes to shop.
       5. She likes to read.
       6. She likes the movies.

   b. 1. It is nice.
       2. There are lakes.
       3. There are tennis courts.
       4. There are three fast-food restaurants.
       5. There is a train station.
       6. There is a newspaper store.
       7. There is no library.
       8. There is nothing downtown.
       9. There is no soccer club.
       10. There are no shopping malls.
       11. There is no movie theater.

2. a. 1. to Outer Creek
   b. 2. in Franklin
   c. 1. in or near Outer Creek
   d. 3. at a fast-food restaurant
   e. 2. at a shopping mall
   f. 2. to a library
   g. 3. at a soccer club
   h. 1. at a newspaper store

3. a. are
   b. sits
   c. don't
   d. is
   e. Does
   f. are
   g. doesn't
   h. likes
   i. is, isn't
   j. has
   k. don't, do

4. a. Are there lakes?
   b. Are there tennis courts?
   c. Are there three fast-food restaurants?
   d. Is there a soccer club?
   e. Are there any shopping malls?
   f. Is there a library?
   g. Is there a train station?
   h. Is there a newspaper store?
   i. Is there a movie theater?

5. a. yes   f. no
   b. yes   g. yes
   c. yes   h. yes
   d. no   i. no
   e. no

6. a. 2   d. 1
      1   2
   b. 1   e. 2
      2   1
   c. 2
      1

7. a. Yes, it does.
   b. Yes, it does.
   c. Yes, it does.
   d. No, it doesn't.
   e. No, it doesn't.
   f. No, it doesn't.
   g. Yes, it does.
   h. Yes, it does.
   i. No, it doesn't.

8. a. Sylvia and Eva in math class.
   b. Sylvia sits next to Eva.
   c. Sylvia doesn't have any work now.
   d. Sylvia and Eva are talking.
   e. Eva has some news.
   f. Eva is moving.
   g. Eva's mother's job is changing.
   h. Eva doesn't want to move.
   i. Eva likes Franklin.

Lesson 6: Anything Else? *page 28*

1. a. 1. He is going to school.
      2. He is wearing a shirt and pants.
      3. He is wearing shoes and socks.
      4. He has an uncle.
      5. His uncle is helping him.
   b. 1. He is helping Larry.
      2. He wants Larry to tuck in his shirt.
      3. He wants Larry to comb his hair.
      4. He wants Larry to put on his sneakers.

2. a. 2. Bob
   b. 1. Larry
   c. 1. tuck it in
   d. 3. comb it
   e. 1. change them
   f. 3. to look better

3. a. tuck in   f. goes
   b. isn't   g. doesn't
   c. Comb   h. does
   d. Don't, have   i. is going
   e. Put on   j. Don't

4. a. What is wrong with his shirt?
   b. What is wrong with his hair?
   c. What is wrong with his shoes?
   d. What is wrong with his socks?
   e. What is wrong with his pants?
   f. What is wrong with his belt?

5. a. yes   d. no
   b. no   e. no
   c. yes   f. no

6. a. 2   d. 1
      1   2
   b. 1   e. 2
      2   1
   c. 2
      1

7. a. Don't put on your blue sneakers.
   b. Don't put on your blue shirt.
   c. Don't put on your blue blouse.
   d. Don't put on your blue tie.
   e. Don't put on your blue shoes.
   f. Don't put on your blue pants.
   g. Don't put on your blue boots.

8. a. He goes to school.
   b. He has an uncle.
   c. His uncle's name is Bob.
   d. Bob is his uncle.
   e. His shirt is out.
   f. His hair doesn't look combed.
   g. He is wearing brown shoes.
   h. He is wearing blue socks.
   i. He is not wearing sneakers.

Lesson 7: Can You Draw a Stegosaurus? *page 32*

1. a. 1. He is drinking iced tea.
      2. He is drawing pictures.
      3. He is sitting in the kitchen.
      4. His aunt's name is Charlotte.
      5. He is having problems with the stegosaurus.
   b. 1. She is sitting in the kitchen.
      2. She cannot draw a stick figure.
      3. She knows a lot about art.
      4. She knows how to make iced tea.
      5. She is helping Victor.
   c. 1. They have small heads.
      2. They have spikes.
      3. They have short legs.

2. a. 2. for a book
   b. 3. the brontosaurus and the tyrannosaurus
   c. 2. tea and water
   d. 3. They are not thin enough.
   e. 2. It is not small enough.
   f. 3. They are not short enough.
   g. 3. nothing

3. a. is
   b. is
   c. is
   d. have
   e. is coming
   f. can't
   g. does
   h. do
   i. are, aren't
   j. look, don't
   k. looks, doesn't

4. a. Is he having a problem with the iced tea?
   b. Is he having a problem with his aunt?
   c. Is he having a problem with the dinosaurs?
   d. Is he having a problem with the brontosaurus?
   e. Is he having a problem with the tyrannosaurus?
   f. Is he having a problem with the stegosaurus?
   g. Is he having a problem with the spikes?
   h. Is he having a problem with the legs?
   i. Is he having a problem with the head?

5. a. no
   b. yes
   c. no
   d. yes
   e. no
   f. yes
   g. no
   h. yes

6. a. 1
      2
   b. 2
      1
   c. 2
      1
   d. 1
      2
   e. 2
      1

7. a. Who is helping him now?
   b. Who is giving him iced tea now?
   c. Who is drinking iced tea now?
   d. Who is drawing dinosaurs now?
   e. What is coming out wrong now?

8. a. Victor is drawing pictures.
   b. Charlotte is Victor's aunt.
   c. Charlotte cannot draw well.
   d. Victor draws well.
   e. Victor is drawing a stegosaurus now.
   f. He is having problems.
   g. A stegosaurus has a small head.
   h. It has spikes.
   i. It has short legs.

Lesson 8: Does the Sun Ever Come Out in Bergen? *page 37*

1. a. 1. He is in Bergen, Norway.
      2. He is Pilar's father.
      3. He is Maria's husband.
   b. 1. She is in Bergen, Norway.
      2. She is Maria's daughter.
      3. She goes for a walk.
      4. She talks to the man at the front desk.

2. a. 2. Willie
   b. 2. rainy
   c. 1. three
   d. 2. the man at the front desk
   e. 1. in a hotel
   f. 3. Pilar and a man
   g. 2. a tourist and a child

3. a. is
   b. is raining
   c. says, rains
   d. Does, come out
   e. meets
   f. talk
   g. asks
   h. answers, don't know

4. a. Who says it is time for Maria to wake up?
   b. Who says it is raining?
   c. Who says Pilar is out for a walk?
   d. Who says it always rains?
   e. Who says there is an old joke?
   f. Who says he doesn't know?
   g. Who says he is eight years old?

5. a. yes   e. no
   b. yes   f. yes
   c. no   g. yes
   d. yes

6. a. 1   d. 2
      2   1
   b. 2   e. 1
      1   2
   c. 1   f. 2
      2   1

7. a. Does Maria ask if the sun is out?
   b. Does Willie tell Maria it is raining?
   c. Does Maria ask where Pilar is?
   d. Does Willie say she is back?
   e. Does Pilar say it is raining again?
   f. Does the man at the front desk say it always rains?
   g. Does he say there is an old joke?
   h. Does the tourist ask if the sun comes out?
   i. Does the boy say he is only eight?

8. a. Willie is waking Maria.
   b. Pilar is out for a walk.
   c. Maria doesn't like rain.
   d. A man is working at the front desk.
   e. He is telling a joke.
   f. It always rains in Bergen.
   g. The sun never comes out in Bergen.
   h. The tourist asks a question.
   i. The boy says he is eight.

Lesson 9: I Am Not Cut Out for Parachuting *page 42*

1. a. 1. He is Jane's brother.
      2. He is over his cold.
      3. He is feeling fine.
      4. He is going parachuting.
      5. He is working.

b. 1. He is Gary's friend.
   2. He likes to watch.
   3. He is talking to Jane.
   4. He is not cut out for parachuting.

c. 1. She is Gary's sister.
   2. She is talking to Daniel.
   3. She asks Daniel to go.
   4. She likes to parachute.

2. a. 3. Gary's friend
   b. 1. Gary
   c. 1. Gary and Jane
   d. 3. tomorrow
   e. 2. two in the afternoon
   f. 2. Daniel
   g. 3. He doesn't like to parachute.
   h. 1. watches from the ground

3. a. feeling
   b. don't, come
   c. like watching
   d. are, going
   e. don't know
   f. has, work
   g. guess
   h. Come
   i. don't like parachuting

4. a. Why doesn't Daniel like parachuting?
   b. Why doesn't Daniel like high places?
   c. Why doesn't Daniel like flying?
   d. Why doesn't Gary like being sick?
   e. Why doesn't Gary like working?
   f. Why doesn't Gary like being at home?
   g. Why doesn't Jane like working?
   h. Why doesn't Jane like being on the ground?
   i. Why doesn't Jane like watching?

5. a. yes   e. no
   b. no   f. yes
   c. yes   g. yes
   d. yes   h. no

6. a. 1   d. 1
      2   2
   b. 1   e. 1
      2   2
   c. 2
      1

7. a. Daniel talks to Jane.
    b. Gary feels fine.
    c. Jane parachutes.
    d. Daniel stays on the ground.
    e. Gary jumps at two.

8. a. Jane is going parachuting.
    b. Gary is going parachuting.
    c. Daniel is not going parachuting.
    d. Daniel likes watching from the ground.
    e. Daniel doesn't jump from airplanes.
    f. Gary has to work.

Lesson 10: Call Back Later *page 47*

1. a. 1. He lives with his mother.
       2. He is at baseball practice.
       3. He gets home at 6:00.
       4. He eats dinner at 6:30.
    b. 1. He is not at Mario's house.
       2. He calls Mario.
       3. He is not at baseball practice.
       4. He takes piano lessons.
       5. He is going to call back at 8:00.

2. a. 1. Mason
    b. 1. yes
    c. 2. at 6:00
    d. 2. at 7:00
    e. 3. at 8:00
    f. 2. at baseball practice
    g. 3. his piano lesson

3. a. is   e. Call
    b. Is   f. have
    c. is   g. is
    d. does, get

4. a. When does Mario have baseball practice?
    b. When does Mario get home?
    c. When does Bill call Mario?
    d. When does Mario have dinner?
    e. When does Bill have dinner?
    f. When does Bill have a piano lesson?
    g. When does Bill talk to Mario?

5. a. no
    b. yes
    c. yes
    d. yes
    e. no

6. a. 2
       1
    b. 1
       2
    c. 1
       2
    d. 1
       2
    e. 2
       1
    f. 2
       1

7. a. No, he plays every Tuesday.
    b. No, he has it every Tuesday.
    c. No, he goes every Tuesday.
    d. No, he has it every Tuesday.
    e. No, he has it every Tuesday.
    f. No, they play every Tuesday.
    g. No, they have it every Tuesday.

8. a. Mario is not at home.
    b. Mario is at baseball practice.
    c. Mario gets home at 6:00.
    d. Mario eats dinner at 6:30.
    e. Bill is calling Mario.
    f. Bill is talking to Mario's mother.
    g. Bill takes piano lessons.
    h. Bill's piano lesson is at 7:00.

Unit 2

Lesson 11: I Ate Too Much Pizza page 55

1.
   a. Did it rain?
   b. Did Jenny go out for breakfast?
   c. Did she eat breakfast at home?
   d. Did her aunt have breakfast with her?
   e. Did they go out for pizza?
   f. Did Jenny eat too much pizza?

2.
   a. yes
   b. yes
   c. yes
   d. yes
   e. no
   f. yes
   g. yes
   h. no
   i. yes
   j. yes
   k. yes

3.
   a. Yes, it did.
   b. No, it didn't.
   c. Yes, she did.
   d. Yes, she did.
   e. Yes, she did.
   f. Yes, they did.
   g. Yes, it did.
   h. Yes, it did.

4.
   a. 1. Did it rain a lot?
   b. 2. Did it rain a lot?
   c. 3. Did it snow?
   d. 1. Did Jenny get up early?
   e. 1. Did Jenny go into the water?
   f. 1. Did Jenny go out for breakfast?
   g. 1. Did Jenny's cousins come to her house?
   h. 2. Did the sun come out?

5.
   a. didn't she?
   b. didn't she?
   c. didn't they?
   d. didn't she?
   e. didn't it?
   f. didn't it?
   g. didn't they?
   h. didn't she?

6. a. 1. Yes, it did.
   b. 2. No, she didn't.
   c. 2. No, she had it for lunch.
   d. 3. Yes, they did.
   e. 1. Yes, it did.
   f. 2. No, she didn't.
   g. 2. Yes, they did.

7. a. Visitors came to Jenny's house.
   b. It rained.
   c. Jenny had breakfast.
   d. Jenny ate too much.
   e. Jenny went to the beach.
   f. Li Za went swimming.

Lesson 12: I Got a Cordless Phone for $6.99! *page 59*

1. a. Who went to the store?
   b. Who just came home?
   c. Who told Roberta about the sale?
   d. Who read about it?
   e. Who got a phone?
   f. Who bought a phone before?
   g. Who made a mistake?
   h. Who left the phone in the car?

2. a. yes   e. yes
   b. yes   f. no
   c. no   g. no
   d. no

3. a. Walter did.   e. Roberta did.
   b. Walter did.   f. Walter did.
   c. Walter did.   g. Roberta did.
   d. Suzie did.   h. Walter did.

4. a. 1. Who went shopping?
   b. 2. Did he buy a phone?
   c. 1. Who told Roberta about the sale?
   d. 3. Did Roberta read about it?
   e. 2. Who got a cordless phone?
   f. 1. Who paid $6.99?
   g. 3. Did Roberta get mad?
   h. 2. Who made a mistake?

5. a. Roberta didn't go to Gil's, did she?
   No, she didn't.
   b. Suzie didn't buy one, did she?
   No, she didn't.
   c. Walter didn't tell her, did he?
   No, he didn't.
   d. Roberta didn't get one, did she?
   No, she didn't.
   e. Walter didn't read about it, did he?
   No, he didn't.
   f. Suzie didn't get one, did she?
   No, she didn't.
   g. Suzie didn't make one, did she?
   No, she didn't.
   h. Suzie didn't leave it there, did she?
   No, she didn't.

6. a. 3. Walter did.
   b. 2. No, Walter did.
   c. 2. Roberta read about it.
   d. 3. Yes, it did.
   e. 1. Suzie did.
   f. 1. No, it lasted four days.
   g. 3. Walter did.
   h. 2. No, Walter left it there.

7. a. Walter bought a phone for $3.99.
   b. It lasted four days.
   c. Walter bought a cordless phone.
   d. Walter put the phone in the car.
   e. Walter told Roberta he bought a phone.
   f. Roberta got mad.

Lesson 13: Where Did You Buy Your Down Jacket? *page 64*

1. a. What did they have?
   b. Who won?
   c. Was December warm?
   d. Was January warm?
   e. When was the ice storm?
   f. Who saw a sale?

2. a. no			e. no
   b. yes		f. yes
   c. yes		g. yes
   d. no			h. no

3. a. It is choppy.
   b. It was warm.
   c. It was warm.
   d. It was cold.
   e. It is down.
   f. It is blue.
   g. It is large.

4. a. 1. What is the ice like?
   b. 2. Who won?
   c. 1. When was the ice storm?
   d. 3. Where did Ilyan get his jacket?
   e. 2. What is the name of the store?
   f. 1. How much did the jacket cost?
   g. 1. What size is Ilyan?
   h. 3. What color did he send for?
   i. 3. How long did it take to get the jacket?

5. a. Yes it is, and it won before.
   b. Yes he is, and he wore it before.
   c. Yes he is, and he wore one before.
   d. Yes he is, and he ordered from one before.
   e. Yes he is, and he looked at one before.
   f. Yes he is, and he talked about one before.
   g. Yes they are, and they looked at one before.
   h. Yes they are, and they sent away for them before.

6. a. 2. It is choppy.
   b. 3. Great Gulch won.
   c. 3. They were warm.
   d. 2. He took it out last week.
   e. 3. It was last week.
   f. 1. 100%
   g. 1. from The Down Place
   h. 1. $95
   i. 2. 16
   j. 1. It is a blue down jacket.
   k. 3. The Down Place paid.

7. a. Ilyan looked in a catalog.
   b. Ilyan sent away for a jacket.
   c. Ilyan got a small blue jacket.
   d. Ilyan sent back the small blue jacket.
   e. Ilyan got a large green jacket.
   f. Ilyan sent back the large green jacket.
   g. Ilyan got a large blue jacket.
   h. Great Gulch won a hockey game.
   i. Ilyan and Omar went ice-skating.

Lesson 14: How Did You Break Your Elbow? *page 69*

1. a. Who is Nancy's brother?
   b. Where was Bob last night?
   c. What did Nancy break?
   d. Who fell in front of Nancy?
   e. Who smashed into Nancy?
   f. Who skated into Nancy?
   g. Did Nancy sit on the bench?
   h. Whom did Nancy call?
   i. Who came for her?
   j. Who took her to the hospital?

2. a. yes   f. yes
   b. no   g. yes
   c. no   h. no
   d. no   i. no
   e. no   j. yes

3. a. Bob and Robert played hockey last night.
   b. Winnie fell in front of Nancy.
   c. Nancy jumped over Winnie.
   d. Michelle smashed into Nancy.
   e. Lynne skated into Nancy.
   f. Robert came for Nancy.
   g. Nancy's mother took her to the hospital.
   h. Bob broke his wrist.

4. a. 2. Where did Bob hear it?
   b. 2. What did Bob hear?
   c. 1. When did Nancy break her elbow?
   d. 3. Where did Nancy break her elbow?
   e. 3. Where did Nancy sit?
   f. 1. When did Nancy sit on the bench?
   g. 2. Who came for Nancy?
   h. 1. When did Robert come for Nancy?
   i. 2. What couldn't Nancy move?
   j. 2. Where did Nancy's mother take her?

5. a. But I talked.
   b. But I jumped.
   c. But I got up.
   d. But I skated into her.
   e. But I fell.
   f. But I sat on the bench.
   g. But I decided to play.
   h. But I called Robert.
   i. But I came for her.
   j. But I got Chinese food.
   k. But I went home.
   l. But I moved my arm.

6. a. 3. Bob
   b. 2. the night before last
   c. 2. at the beginning of practice
   d. 1. Michelle smashed into Nancy.
   e. 2. Lynne skated into Nancy.
   f. 3. She broke her elbow.
   g. 3. at Lucky Star
   h. 3. to the hospital

7. a. The state champion hit the ball hard.
   b. Bob broke his wrist.
   c. Nancy went to hockey practice.
   d. Nancy called Robert.
   e. Robert picked her up.
   f. They went for Chinese food.
   g. Nancy's mother took her to the hospital.
   h. Bob talked to Robert.

Lesson 15: This Soup Is Awful! Did You Forget the Salt? *page 74*

1. a. Who made lunch?
   b. Who made the salad?
   c. Who made the salad dressing?
   d. Who made the bread?
   e. Who made the soup?
   f. What did Joe make?
   g. What did Gary make?
   h. What did Dad make?
   i. What did Dorothy make?
   j. What did Gary put in the soup?
   k. What did Joe put in the salad?

2. a. yes   e. yes
   b. no   f. no
   c. yes   g. no
   d. no   h. no

3. a. They made lunch.
   b. He made the salad.
   c. He made the soup.
   d. He made the salad dressing.
   e. She made the bread.
   f. He put in all the vegetables he could find.

4. a. 2. What did Joe put in the salad?
   b. 1. What came from the garden?
   c. 3. What came from a can?
   d. 1. What came from downtown?
   e. 2. What came from across the street?
   f. 1. What didn't Joe like?
   g. 3. What did Gary put in the soup?

5. a. What did they make?
   b. What did he make?
   c. What did he make?
   d. What did he make?
   e. What did they put in the salad?
   f. What did they use in the salad?
   g. What did they add to the salad?
   h. What did they throw in?
   i. What did they have with lunch?
   j. What did Dorothy make?

6. a. 2. No, he didn't.
   b. 1. the soup
   c. 3. the bread
   d. 1. vegetables and cheese
   e. 2. They made lunch.
   f. 2. the ones from the garden
   g. 3. the cheese from downtown
   h. 2. some from a can

7. a. Dad made salad dressing.
   b. Dorothy made bread.
   c. Gary passed Joe a bowl of soup.
   d. Joe took some bread.
   e. Joe tried the soup.
   f. Joe asked for the salt.

Unit 3

Lesson 16: I Won't Be Back until August *page 81*

1.
   - a. yes
   - b. no
   - c. no
   - d. no
   - e. no
   - f. yes
   - g. yes
   - h. yes
   - i. yes
   - j. yes
   - k. yes

2.
   - a. 1. Wendy
   - b. 1. in June
   - c. 3. Yes, there is.
   - d. 2. the swim meet
   - e. 2. July 25
   - f. 3. in August
   - g. 1. Wendy
   - h. 3. by plane
   - i. 1. in a supermarket

3. The following locations should be numbered on the map:
   1—Lake Michigan
   2—Oregon
   3—New Orleans
   Arrows should be drawn from the **1** to the **2** and from the **2** to the **3**.

4.
   - a. Lake Michigan/sailing
   - b. July
   - c. New Orleans
   - d. August 15
   - e. tennis games
   - f. July 4
   - g. swim meet
   - h. July 25

5.
   - a. No, she is saying good-bye tomorrow.
   - b. No, she is coming back tomorrow.
   - c. No, she is going to the swim meet tomorrow.
   - d. No, she is going sailing tomorrow.
   - e. No, she is going camping tomorrow.
   - f. No, she is flying to New Orleans tomorrow.
   - g. No, she is seeing her uncle tomorrow.

6.
   - a. No, I won't play tennis until August.
   - b. No, I won't go swimming until August.
   - c. No, I won't go sailing until August.
   - d. No, I won't go to Oregon until August.

Lesson 17: You Don't Play Football! *page 85*

1. a. yes
   b. no
   c. yes
   d. yes
   e. yes
   f. no
   g. no
   h. yes
   i. no

2. a. 1. to football practice
   b. 2. take pictures
   c. 2. before dinner
   d. 2. after football practice
   e. 1. before 5:45
   f. 1. at 5:45
   g. 3. at dinner
   h. 3. at 6:00

3. The following locations should be numbered on the map:
   1—David's house
   2—the football field
   3—Bundy's Chicken
   Arrows should be drawn from the **1** to the **2**, from the **2** to the **3**, and from the **3** to the **1**.

4. a. football practice/take pictures
   b. Bundy's/pick up chicken
   c. home/dinner
   d. call Bundy's/order chicken
   e. home/dinner

5. a. No, he is going to play now.
   b. No, he is going to take pictures now.
   c. No, he is going to have chicken now.
   d. No, he is going to pick it up now.
   e. No, he is going to eat now.
   f. No, she is going to call now.
   g. No, she is going to order it now.
   h. No, he is going to pay for it now.

6. a. No, he won't go until 4:30.
   b. No, he won't play until 4:30.
   c. No, he won't take pictures until 4:30.
   d. No, he won't have dinner until 4:30.
   e. No, he won't eat until 4:30.
   f. No, she won't call until 4:30.
   g. No, he won't pay for it until 4:30.
   h. No, he won't pick it up until 4:30.
   i. No, they won't have fried chicken until 4:30.

Lesson 18: I'm Going to Quit *page 88*

1. a. yes
   b. yes
   c. yes
   d. no
   e. yes
   f. no
   g. yes
   h. yes

2. a. 1. Tom
   b. 3. Kevin
   c. 2. next Thursday
   d. 2. Jason and Kevin
   e. 1. Marla
   f. 2. Tom
   g. 1. Marla
   h. 1. Marla
   i. 3. many tennis players
   j. 1. Tom

3. a. Marla
   b. Tom
   c. Marla
   d. Tom
   e. Marla
   f. Marla
   g. Tom
   h. Marla

4. a. mad.
   b. lose.
   c. win.
   d. have a chance.
   e. start playing.
   f. have a better chance.
   g. find another tennis player.
   h. find one.

5. a. No, she didn't. But she will.
   b. No, he didn't. But he will.
   c. No, they didn't. But they will.
   d. No, they didn't. But they will.
   e. No, he didn't. But he will.
   f. No, he didn't. But he will.
   g. No, she didn't. But she will.
   h. No, they didn't. But they will.
   i. No, he didn't. But he will.
   j. No, they didn't. But they will.

6. a. No, and she isn't going to, either.
   b. No, and they aren't going to, either.
   c. No, and he isn't going to, either.
   d. No, and they aren't going to, either.
   e. No, and they aren't going to, either.
   f. No, and they aren't going to, either.
   g. No, and he isn't going to, either.
   h. No, and he isn't going to, either.
   i. No, and she isn't going to, either.

Lesson 19: Are You Going to Go Back to Your Country? *page 92*

1. a. yes   f. yes
   b. no   g. yes
   c. no   h. no
   d. no   i. yes
   e. yes   j. yes

2. a. 1. in his class
   b. 3. to his country
   c. 1. to Texas
   d. 2. in art
   e. 1. in Texas
   f. 1. to Texas
   g. 2. to his class in the United States
   h. 2. to art

3. a. They are talking in school.
   b. They are going to art.
   c. He will go back to his country.
   d. He will be with his family in his country.
   e. She will work in Texas.
   f. They will go to Texas.
   g. He is going to art.

4. Letters **b, c,** and **d** should be **circled**. Plans **a** and **e** should be crossed out.

5. a. No, he is going to clean it off next week.
   b. No, they are going to line up next week.
   c. No, she is going to talk to him next week.
   d. No, he is going to go back next week.
   e. No, he is going to go to art next week.
   f. No, he is going to send them a postcard next week.

6. a. No, but he will be.
    b. No, but they will be.
    c. No, but they will be.
    d. No, but there will be.
    e. No, but he will be.
    f. No, but she will be.
    g. No, but they will be.
    h. No, but he will be.
    i. No, but he will be.

Lesson 20: Why Won't You Lend Me Three Thousand Dollars? *page 95*

1. a. no   g. no
    b. yes   h. yes
    c. no   i. no
    d. no   j. yes
    e. no   k. no
    f. yes

2. a. 3. go to Nassau
    b. 2. pay his father back
    c. 2. to Nassau
    d. 3. $3,000
    e. 2. Bob owes his father.
    f. 2. Bob
    g. 2. Bob
    h. 3. their father
    i. 1. Allan

3. Letters **a** and **c** should be **circled**. Letters **b, d, e, f, g, h, i, j, k,** and **l** should be **crossed out with an X**.

4. a. no   g. no
    b. no   h. yes
    c. no   i. no
    d. yes   j. no
    e. yes   k. maybe
    f. no

5. a. No, but he is going to go to Nassau in five weeks.
   b. No, but he is going to lend Bob money in five weeks.
   c. No, but he is going to borrow money in five weeks.
   d. No, but he is going to borrow money in five weeks.
   e. No, but he is going to call him in five weeks.
   f. No, but he is going to borrow $3,000 in five weeks.
   g. No, but he is going to pay it back in five weeks.

6. a. No, he didn't. But he is going to.
   b. No, they didn't. But they are going to.
   c. No, he didn't. But he is going to.
   d. No, she didn't. But she is going to.
   e. No, she didn't. But she is going to.
   f. No, he didn't. But he is going to.
   g. No, they didn't. But they are going to.
   h. No, she didn't. But she is going to.
   i. No, he didn't. But he is going to.
   j. No, we didn't. But we are going to.

Unit 4

Lesson 21: We Got a New Teacher Yesterday *page 101*

1. a. education
   b. probably
   c. important
   d. miss
   e. company
   f. director
   g. training
   h. ugly
   i. forgot

2. a. forgot
   b. director
   c. miss
   d. probably
   e. training
   f. important
   g. company
   h. ugly
   i. education

3. a. Tina and Anabel are talking on the phone.
   b. Tina's class has a new teacher.
   c. Tina and Anabel are going to the movies.
   d. Ms. Chin was Tina's teacher.
   e. Ms. Chin knows a lot about education.
   f. Tina's new teacher is probably a good teacher.

4. a. talk
   b. forgot
   c. got
   d. happened
   e. got
   f. knows
   g. is
   h. tell
   i. likes

5. a. 3. going to the movies
   b. 2. She got a new job.
   c. 3. at a computer company
   d. 3. teaching and learning
   e. 1. He isn't good-looking.
   f. 1. No, she doesn't.
   g. 3. nobody
   h. 1. They want her to come back.

6. a. F
   b. T
   c. T
   d. F
   e. T
   f. T
   g. F
   h. T

103

7. a. 1. We can talk more about it.
   b. 2. I forgot to tell you.
   c. 3. She got a new job.
   d. 3. She knows a lot about training.
   e. 3. He is probably a good teacher.
   f. 1. We all miss Ms. Chin.

8. g.   f.
   e.   a.
   i.   h.
   d.   c.
   b.

9. Answers will vary.

10. Answers will vary.

Lesson 22: I Came to Register My Brother *page 107*

1. a. adults   c. official
   b. records   d. register

2. a. register   d. official
   b. adults   e. adults
   c. records

3. a. Rafael speaks English.
   b. Rafael and Guillermo's father doesn't speak English.
   c. Guillermo came to register for school.
   d. Guillermo's brother is Rafael.
   e. Guillermo went to school in Spain.
   f. Guillermo studied English in Spain.
   g. Guillermo came here three days ago.

4. a. came   g. had
   b. is   h. took
   c. talk   i. give
   d. is   j. wants
   e. did   k. do
   f. gave

5. a. 2. two
    b. 3. twelve
    c. 3. three
    d. 3. three days ago
    e. 2. his father and brother
    f. 3. in the library
    g. 2. Monday through Thursday
    h. 1. nothing
    i. 3. at 9:00

6. a. F   e. T
    b. T   f. T
    c. F   g. T
    d. F   h. F

7. a. 1. This is my father.
    b. 1. He doesn't speak English.
    c. 2. They are sending you the official ones.
    d. 1. Fill out these forms.
    e. 3. Tell your father we are happy he is here.
    f. 3. He can go to classes if he wants to.
    g. 3. They meet in the library on Monday, Tuesday, Wednesday, and Thursday.
    h. 1. They are free.

8. b.   g.
    f.   e.
    h.   a.
    d.   i.
    j.   c.

9. Answers will vary.

10. Answers will vary.

Lesson 23: Are You Going to Buy a Wheelchair or Rent One? *page 114*

1. a. landed   e. rent
    b. expensive   f. injured
    c. wheelchair   g. mess
    d. jump shot

2. a. expensive
   b. rent
   c. mess
   d. wheelchair
   e. jump shot
   f. injured
   g. landed

3. a. He fell at a basketball game.
   b. He broke his leg when he fell.
   c. He was in bed for two days.
   d. He is coming to Luke's house when he leaves the hospital.
   e. He will be walking in a month.
   f. He is going back home when he is better.
   g. He went to County Hospital after he fell.

4. a. happened
   b. went
   c. made
   d. landed
   e. injured
   f. walk
   g. coming
   h. rent
   i. says
   j. coming
   k. happened

5. a. 2. at a basketball game
   b. 1. after a jump shot
   c. 2. for two days
   d. 2. when he leaves the hospital
   e. 1. in a month
   f. 1. in Manchester
   g. 3. in Black Ridge
   h. 3. at Luke's house

6. a. F
   b. F
   c. T
   d. F
   e. T
   f. T
   g. T
   h. T
   i. F
   j. T

7. a. 1. He can't walk.
   b. 2. He went for a jump shot.
   c. 1. He broke his leg in two places.
   d. 2. Can he walk?
   e. 3. He will be walking in a month.
   f. 2. Why is he staying here?
   g. 3. Can't he stay home?

8. b.   e.
   d.   c.
   f.   a.
   g.

9. Answers will vary.

10. Answers will vary.

Lesson 24: If You Don't Open Your Mouth and Answer Me, I'm Leaving!
page 120

1. a. glad   d. just
   b. type   e. kidding
   c. report   f. typewriter

2. a. typewriter   d. kidding
   b. report   e. just
   c. glad   f. type

3. a. Howard is Don's brother.
   b. Don has a report to type.
   c. Don wants Howard's help.
   d. Don is not kidding.
   e. Don helped Howard in February.
   f. Don and Howard have a word processor.
   g. Don says he will leave.

4. a. glad   f. do
   b. want   g. word processor
   c. type   h. typewriter
   d. help   i. open
   e. report

5. a. 2. Don
   b. 2. Don
   c. 2. Don
   d. 2. Don helped Howard.
   e. 1. Howard
   f. 2. Don

6. a. T   e. F
   b. T   f. F
   c. F   g. T
   d. F   h. T

7. a. 1. I'm glad you are home.
    b. 2. You are just the person I want to see.
    c. 3. How come?
    d. 3. Are you kidding?
    e. 2. You can help me.
    f. 3. What is there to think about?
    g. 1. You do twenty-five, I do fifty.
    h. 2. You use the word processor.

8. c.   a.
    g.   d.
    b.   f.
    i.   e.
    h.

9. Answers will vary.

10. Answers will vary.

Lesson 25: A Pain in My Shoulder, an Earache, and My Arm Hurts *page 126*

1. a. visit   e. shoulder
    b. stoplight   f. in the rear
    c. patient   g. appointment
    d. side   h. earache

2. a. earache   e. visit
    b. in the rear   f. patient
    c. side   g. shoulder
    d. stoplight   h. appointment

3. a. Her name is Dr. Rubin.
    b. He has a pain in his shoulder, an earache, and his arm hurts.
    c. His name is Pete Caravella.
    d. His telephone number at home is 555-7622.
    e. Her address is 2811 Plaque Boulevard.

4. a. see   h. visit
    b. patient   i. 555-7622
    c. shoulder   j. 302
    d. earache   k. Right
    e. Thursday   l. left
    f. 10:00   m. right
    g. Tuesday

5. a. 2. Dr. Rubin
   b. 1. an earache
   c. 1. Pete Caravella
   d. 2. 555-7622
   e. 3. 555-4800, extension 302
   f. 2. 2811 Plaque Boulevard

6. a. T   e. T
   b. F   f. F
   c. F   g. F
   d. T

7. a. 2. I want to see Dr. Rubin.
   b. 1. Thursday Morning at 9:45
   c. 3. next Monday at 6:00
   d. 3. What is the problem?
   e. 2. What is your telephone number?
   f. 1. Where is your office?

8. f.   g.
   c.   a.
   b.   e.
   d.

9. Answers will vary.

10. Answers will vary.

Lesson 26: I Won't Say Hello Because She Never Says Hello *page 133*

1. a. storeroom   d. attitude
   b. be crazy about   e. boss
   c. auto parts   f. shelves

2. a. shelves   d. attitude
   b. auto parts   e. storeroom
   c. boss   f. be crazy about

3. a. She works in an auto parts store.
   b. He works in an auto parts store.
   c. Michelle and Kenneth work for Lynn.
   d. Lynn is the boss.
   e. The store always looks good.
   f. She likes their work.
   g. She doesn't like Kenneth's attitude.
   h. He keeps the shelves full and the storeroom clean.

4. a. saw
    b. likes
    c. do
    d. find
    e. smile
    f. shop
    g. gave
    h. say
    i. says

5. a. 3. at an auto parts store
    b. 3. Lynn
    c. 3. Lynn
    d. 3. Yes, she does.
    e. 2. No, she doesn't.
    f. 1. He works well.
    g. 2. He smiles at shoppers.
    h. 3. Lynn
    i. 2. She never says hello.

6. a. F
    b. F
    c. T
    d. T
    e. F
    f. T
    g. T
    h. T
    i. F
    j. F

7. a. 2. I just saw Lynn.
    b. 3. She is not crazy about your attitude.
    c. 3. Attitude? What attitude?
    d. 1. The shelves are always full.
    e. 2. It is a good place to shop.
    f. 1. I saw hello to everyone.
    g. 1. She doesn't shop here.
    h. 2. She gave you the job.
    i. 3. You say hello first.

8. d.
    e.
    c.
    b.
    a.
    h.
    f.
    g.

9. Answers will vary.

10. Answers will vary.

Lesson 27: Did You Read the Book I Gave You? *page 140*

1. a. hurry up
   b. garage
   c. dinner
   d. waiting
   e. copy
   f. evening

2. a. waiting
   b. evening
   c. copy
   d. dinner
   e. hurry up
   f. garage

3. a. They are having lunch.
   b. He gave it to her two days ago.
   c. She went skating two nights ago.
   d. She played tennis after school yesterday.
   e. She went out for dinner last night.
   f. She played soccer last night.
   g. No, she didn't.
   h. Yes, she does.
   i. Yes, he does.
   j. She will read the book tomorrow.

4. a. read
   b. went
   c. dinner
   d. think
   e. hurry up
   f. copy
   g. painting
   h. will
   i. want
   j. have

5. a. 3. He wants her to read it.
   b. 3. She didn't have time.
   c. 2. It is a good book.
   d. 1. They have many things to do.
   e. 3. by Monday
   f. 1. He wants to go to the movies with her.
   g. 3. She has to read the book.

6. a. T
   b. T
   c. F
   d. T
   e. T
   f. T
   g. T
   h. F
   i. F
   j. T

7. a. 1. Did you read the book?
   b. 1. I got it two days ago.
   c. 2. I went skating that night.
   d. 3. I had dinner out with my uncle.
   e. 1. When did you think I was going to read?
   f. 3. Give it to them first.
   g. 3. Jeff and Joe are painting their uncle's house.
   h. 2. I will finish it by Monday.
   i. 1. I have to read a book.

8. h.   f.
   d.   b.
   i.   g.
   e.   c.
   a.

9. Answers will vary.

10. Answers will vary.

Lesson 28: Did You Tell Them We Are Not Inviting Them? *page 146*

1. a. neighbors   d. salad
   b. next door   e. make it
   c. how about   f. inviting

2. a. make it   d. next door
   b. inviting   e. how about
   c. neighbors   f. salad

3. a. The party is from 7:00 to 11:00.
   b. The party is Sunday.
   c. Sheridan and Alistair are having a party.
   d. The party is at their house.
   e. They are going to make sandwiches and salad.
   f. They are going to buy drinks, fruit, and ice cream.
   g. They don't want to invite the Hansens.

4. a. want   e. inviting
   b. How about   f. next door
   c. buy   g. have
   d. How about   h. get

5. a. 2. 7:00 to 11:00
   b. 2. Sunday
   c. 3. Monday is a holiday.
   d. 2. sandwiches and a salad
   e. 2. drinks and ice cream
   f. 2. at Hansen's Ice Cream Store
   g. 2. No, they aren't.
   h. 2. next door
   i. 2. Sunday

6. a. F   f. F
   b. T   g. F
   c. F   h. T
   d. T   i. T
   e. F

Answer Key, Lesson 29   113

7. a. 1. What time do you want to tell people to come?
    b. 3. Let's make it at 7:00.
    c. 1. How about Sunday? Monday is a holiday.
    d. 2. We can buy drinks, fruit, and ice cream.
    e. 1. We aren't inviting them.
    f. 3. I will get it Sunday afternoon.

8. b.   g.
    d.   h.
    f.   e.
    a.   c.

9. Answers will vary.

10. Answers will vary.

Lesson 29: Did She Say Why She Is Moving? *page 153*

1. a. of course   e. moving
    b. packing   f. concert
    c. miss   g. art show
    d. private school

2. a. packing   e. moving
    b. art show   f. concert
    c. private school   g. miss
    d. of course

3. a. Julia is going to move.
    b. She is home packing.
    c. She is going to live at her parents' school.
    d. No, she won't.
    e. She is moving the day after tomorrow.
    f. Everybody will miss her.

4. a. see   e. going
    b. moving   f. is
    c. art show   g. going
    d. say

5. a. 3. in her house
    b. 1. in two days
    c. 2. on Thursday
    d. 3. on Sunday
    e. 1. Her parents have a school.
    f. 1. at the school
    g. 1. over the mountain
    h. 2. in the northern United States

6. a. F   e. T
    b. F   f. F
    c. T   g. F
    d. T   h. T

7. a. 1. She is home packing.
    b. 2. At 2:00 tomorrow.
    c. 2. He won't be here.
    d. 1. She will miss the Sunday concert.
    e. 2. Her parents run a private school.
    f. 2. Does she want to?
    g. 3. Are you going to miss her?
    h. 1. So is everybody.

8. d.   b.
    e.   h.
    a.   g.
    f.   c.

9. Answers will vary.

10. Answers will vary.

Lesson 30: The Winter County Free Public Library *page 159*

1. a. library card   d. upstairs
    b. photocopy machine   e. dollar changer
    c. permanent   f. temporary

2. a. dollar changer   d. photocopy machine
    b. library card   e. permanent
    c. temporary   f. upstairs

3. a. He is at the library.
    b. He lives in Rossburg.
    c. It is behind the children's section.
    d. It is next to the photocopy machine.

4. a. library   e. card
    b. name   f. days
    c. address   g. upstairs
    d. number   h. machine

5.
   a. 1. a library card
   b. 2. in Rossburg
   c. 3. E–R–I–K
   d. 1. 1400 Brook Drive
   e. 3. 320–A
   f. 2. 555–3142
   g. 1. in seven to ten days
   h. 2. by mail
   i. 2. nine to six
   j. 1. Sundays
   k. 3. reading rooms
   l. 2. ten cents
   m. 2. next to the photocopy machine

6.
   a. T
   b. F
   c. T
   d. F
   e. T
   f. T

7.
   a. 2. I need a library card.
   b. 3. Give me your name.
   c. 3. Please tell me your name.
   d. 3. Is there any apartment number there?
   e. 1. What are the library hours?
   f. 2. We're closed Thursdays.
   g. 1. We have a dollar changer.

8.
   c.
   f.
   b.
   e.
   g.
   d.
   a.
   h.

9. Answers will vary.

10. Answers will vary.

NTC ESL/EFL TEXTS AND MATERIAL
Junior High—Adult Education

Computer Software
Amigo
Basic Vocabulary Builder on Computer

Language and Culture Readers
Beginner's English Reader
Cultural Encounters in the U.S.A.
Passport to America series
  California Discovery
  Adventures in the Southwest
  The Coast-to-Coast Mystery
  The New York Connection
Discover America series
(text/audiocassettes)
  California
  Chicago
  Florida
  Hawaii
  New England
  New York
  Texas
  Washington, D.C.
Looking at American Signs
Looking at American Food
Looking at American Recreation
Looking at American Holidays
Time: We the People (text/audiocassettes)

Text/Audiocassette Learning Packages
Speak Up! Sing Out! 1, 2
Listen and Say It Right in English!

Transparencies
Everyday Situations in English

Duplicating Masters and Blackline Masters
Easy Vocabulary Games
Vocabulary Games
Advanced Vocabulary Games
Play and Practice!
Basic Vocabulary Builder
Practical Vocabulary Builder
Beginning Activities for English
  Language Learners
Intermediate Activities for English
  Language Learners
Advanced Activities for English
  Language Learners

Language-Skills Texts
English with a Smile 1, 2
English Survival Series
  Building Vocabulary A, B, C
  Recognizing Details A, B, C
  Identifying Main Ideas A, B, C
  Writing Sentences and Paragraphs
    A, B, C
  Using the Context A, B, C
English Across the Curriculum 1, 2, 3
Essentials of Reading and Writing
  English 1, 2, 3
Everyday English 1, 2, 3, 4
Learning to Listen in English
  (workbook/audiocassettes)
Listening to Communicate in English
  (workbook/audiocassettes)
Communication Skillbooks 1, 2, 3
Living in the U.S.A. 1, 2, 3
Basic Everyday Spelling Workbook
  (audiocassettes)
Practical Everyday Spelling Workbook
  (audiocassettes)
Advanced Readings and Conversations
Practical English Writing Skills
Express Yourself in Written English
Campus English
Speak English!
Read English!
Write English!
Orientation in American English
Building English Sentences
Grammar for Use
Grammar Step-by-Step
Listening by Doing
Reading by Doing
Speaking by Doing
Vocabulary by Doing
Writing by Doing
Look, Think and Write

Survival-Skills Texts
Building Real Life English Skills
Everyday Consumer English
Book of Forms
Essential Life Skills series
Finding a Job in the United States
English for Adult Living 1, 2
Living in English
Prevocational English

TOEFL Preparation
NTC's Preparation Course for the
  TOEFL® (with 3 audiocassettes)
NTC's Practice Tests for the TOEFL®
  (with 3 audiocassettes)

Dictionaries and References
ABC's of Languages and Linguistics
Everyday American English Dictionary
Building Dictionary Skills in
  English (workbook)
Beginner's Dictionary of American
  English Usage
Beginner's English Dictionary
  Workbook
NTC's American Idioms Dictionary
NTC's Dictionary of American Slang
  and Colloquial Expressions
Essential American Idioms
Contemporary American Slang
Forbidden American English
101 American English Idioms
Idiom Workbook
Essentials of English Grammar
The Complete ESL/EFL Resource Book
Safari Grammar
Safari Punctuation
303 Dumb Spelling Mistakes
TESOL Professional Anthologies
  Grammar and Composition
  Listening, Speaking, and Reading
  Culture

For further information or a current catalog, write:
National Textbook Company
a division of *NTC Publishing Group*
4255 West Touhy Avenue
Lincolnwood, Illinois 60646-1975 U.S.A.